The

The First Well

A
Bethlehem
Boyhood

Jabra Ibrahim Jabra

Translated by
Issa J. Boullata

The University of Arkansas Press
Fayetteville   1995

First published in Arabic in Great Britain as *al-Bi'r al-Ula*
Copyright © 1987 Riad El-Rayyes Books Ltd. (London)

English translation copyright 1995 by the Board of Trustees
of the University of Arkansas
All rights reserved
Manufactured in the United States of America

99   98   97   96   95   5   4   3   2   1

Designed by Gail Carter

☉ The paper used in this publication meets the minimum
requirements of the American National Standard for Perma-
nence of Paper for Printed Library Materials Z39.48-1984.

Library of Congress Cataloging-in-Publication Data

Jabrā, Jabrā Ibrāhīm.
    [Bi'r al-ūlá.   English]
    The first well : a Bethlehem boyhood / Jabra Ibrahim Jabra ;
    translated by Issa J. Boullata.
        p.   cm.
    ISBN 1-55728-349-4 (cloth : alk. paper). —
    ISBN 1-55728-381-8 (paper : alk. paper)
    1. Jabrā, Jabrā Ibrāhīm—Biography.   2. Authors, Arab—
    Palestine—Biography.   3. Authors, Arab—20th century—
    Biography.   I. Title.
    PJ7840.A322Z46813   1995
    892'.7809—dc20
    [B]   95-18662
                                                        CIP

This translation is dedicated

to the memory of

Ann Munton

and

Jabra Ibrahim Jabra

Translator's Preface

Jabra Ibrahim Jabra was one of the leading writers of the Arab world. A multitalented and creative intellectual, he was a novelist, a short-story writer, a poet, a literary and art critic, an essayist, and a translator of several of Shakespeare's plays and sonnets and over thirty Western literary classics by a variety of other authors, including works by William Faulkner, Samuel Beckett, Edmund Wilson, Jan Kott, and James Frazer. A Palestinian born in Bethlehem on August 28, 1920, he wrote for almost half a century and steadily influenced Arabic literature, art, and thought in the direction of innovation and modernity.

The First Well: A Bethlehem Boyhood tells of Jabra's early years up to the age of twelve. The story mostly takes place in Bethlehem, where he grew up and went to school, but it also takes place in Jerusalem, where his family moved and where he continued his education. Originally published in Arabic by Riad El-Rayyes Books Ltd. of London in 1987 under the title of *al-Bi'r al-Ula* (*The First Well*), it is beautifully written and captures with rare sensitivity not only the historical atmosphere of a period, but also the insights into the boy who would later become the man. Wordsworth's saying, "The Child is father of the Man," could not be truer than it is in this autobiography, which chronicles Jabra's literary and artistic interests from an early age as he grew up in poor family conditions and which describes the boyhood experiences whose social, psychological, and spiritual impact remained with him all his life.

The First Well is a good introduction to understanding the well-known writer Jabra has become. His prodigious memory and strong power of observation that served him so well as a writer, particularly in fiction and poetry, are omnipresent in this outstanding autobiography.

A graduate of the Arab College in Jerusalem in 1937, Jabra won a scholarship to study English literature in England, where he earned a bachelor of arts in 1943 and a master of arts in 1948 at Fitzwilliam House, Cambridge University. On his return to Palestine, he taught English literature at his former school in Jerusalem, the Rashidiyya Secondary School, from 1943 till the end of the British mandate in 1948. Having lost his home in the 1948 fighting that ended in the partial loss of Palestine by the Arabs, he was forced into exile and went to Iraq, where he taught English literature at the College of Arts of the University of Baghdad (1948–1952), then received a two-year research fellowship in the United States at Harvard University (1952–1954). He was later appointed head of publications at the Iraq Petroleum Company in Baghdad (1954–1977), then cultural counselor at the Iraqi Ministry of Culture and Information until he retired in 1984. He died on December 12, 1994, in Baghdad.

Surakh fi Layl Tawil (*Screaming in a Long Night*), written in Jerusalem in 1946 and published in Beirut in 1955, was his first attempt at long fiction. Among his novels, *Hunters in a Narrow Street* was originally published in English (London: Heinemann, 1960) before it was translated into Arabic by Muhammad ʿAsfour in 1973. His novel, *al-Safina* (Beirut, 1970), was translated into English by Roger Allen and Adnan Haydar (*The Ship;* Washington, D.C.: Three Continents Press, 1985). His other novels include *al-Bahth ʿan Waleed Mas ʿoud* (*In Search of Waleed Mas ʿoud;* Beirut, 1978); ʿ*Alam bila Kharaʾit* (*A World without Maps;* Beirut, 1982) authored with ʿAbd al-Rahman Munif; *al-Ghuraf al-Ukhra* (*The Other Rooms;* Beirut, 1986); and *Yawmiyyat Sarab ʿAffan* (*Sarab ʿAffan's Diaries;* London, 1992). "The Gramophone," from his collection ʿ*Arak wa Qisas Ukhra* (*Arak and Other Stories;* Beirut, 1956), was translated by Denys Johnson-Davies and published in his *Modern Arabic Short Stories* (London: Oxford University Press, 1967). Both in his novels and in his short stories, Jabra concentrates on people in Arab cities, their problems and challenges. Sometimes drawn from the poor class, but more often from a rising bourgeoisie and a declining urban elite of tribal origin, his characters are in search of their identity and are mostly in conflict with forces that mercilessly oppress them; hence, the feeling of siege and the need to break out of it in his fiction.

Jabra's poetry, like his fiction, reflects his search for an understanding of the human condition in modern times, with particular emphasis on the growing Arab city caught up in forces that tend to crush its individuals and old venerated values as it moves toward modern urban development. *Tammuz fi al-Madina* (*Tammuz in the City;* Beirut, 1959), his first collection, laments the prevailing spiritual death in the city that needs Tammuz's revivifying force to bring back life and fertility. His second collection, *al-Madar al-Mughlaq* (*The Vicious Circle;* Beirut, 1964), condemns city constraints that choke people's real voices, and it calls for breaking out of its vicious circle. *Lawᶜat al-Shams* (*The Anguish of the Sun;* Baghdad, 1978) proposes love as the only redeeming power that can free humans enslaved by the evils of city life. Many of Jabra's poems have been rendered into English and published in some of the recent well-known anthologies of Arabic poetry in translation.*

Jabra's book, *A Celebration of Life* (Baghdad: Dar al-Ma'mun, 1988), collects his essays originally written in English, some of which are on literary and art criticism. However, most of his literary criticism is in Arabic and is found in books like *al-Hurriyya wa al-Tufan* (*Freedom and the Flood;* Beirut, 1960), *al-Rihla al-Thamina* (*The Eighth Voyage;* Beirut, 1967), *al-Nar wa al-Jawhar* (*Fire and Genuine Essence;* Beirut, 1975), *Yanabiᶜ al-Ru'ya* (*Fountains of Vision;* Beirut, 1979), and others. His English studies in art and art history include *Art in Iraq Today* (Baghdad, 1961), *Contemporary Iraqi Art* (Baghdad, 1972), and *The Grass Roots of Iraqi Art* (Baghdad, 1972). His Arabic ones include *al-Fann wa al-Hulm wa al-Fiᶜl* (*Art, Dream, and Action;* Baghdad, 1985) and *Jawad*

---

*See John Mikhail Asfour, *When the Words Burn* (Ontario: Dunvegan, 1988); Issa J. Boullata, *Modern Arab Poets* (Washington, D.C., 1976); Salma Khadra Jayyusi, *Anthology of Modern Palestinian Literature* (New York, 1992); Mounah A. Khouri and Hamid Algar, *An Anthology of Modern Arabic Poetry* (Berkeley, 1974); Abdullah al-Udhari, *Modern Poetry of the Arab World* (Harmondsworth, 1986).

Salim wa Nusb al-Hurriyya (*Jawad Salim and the Freedom Monument;*
Baghdad, 1974).

Both in art criticism and in literary criticism, Jabra hails the
new, the innovative, when it brings with it a profound vision of
modern life and expresses it creatively with a celebration of
freedom. His aim is always to recognize what helps Arab culture
to become modern without losing its roots in the great accom-
plishments of its past. He wants Arabs to contribute to modern
civilization by creative addition to it, not by imitation of anyone
in the past or the present.

■ ■ ■

Ideas and attitudes like these are foreshadowed in the life
the boy Jabra led in Bethlehem and Jerusalem, which was later
to be enriched by further education and experience. *The First
Well* portrays the budding of the boy's mind and the growth of
his consciousness of life's forces.*

It has been a great pleasure for me to translate this autobiography into English. In this task, which had Jabra's blessing
and approval, I was fortunate to have persons who were willing
to read my translation and make suggestions regarding its
style. First and foremost is Jabra himself, who patiently read
my manuscript in batches. I mailed the batches to him from
Montreal as my translation of the text progressed. The entire
manuscript was mailed back to me just before Desert Storm
wreaked havoc on Baghdad and the Iraqi people in January
1991. Second was Ann Munton, professor of English at the
University of British Columbia in Vancouver, who read the first
seven chapters of my translation but was unable to continue
because of ill health and subsequent death in September 1990.
Last but not least is my wife, Marita Seward Boullata, whose
help and support, as always, have been indispensable, especially
in the preparation of the final version of this translation.

---

*Jabra's second volume of his autobiography, *Shari^c al-Amirat* (*Princesses Street;*
Beirut, 1994), deals mostly with the year 1951 in which he met his beloved
wife, Lami^ca, in Baghdad.

At Jabra's request, I abandoned all diacritics in transliterating Arabic words and proper names, in an effort to make them easier to read, and I often adopted his suggested spelling of them, thus Susan (not Sawsan) and Lameece (not Lamīs). There is some inconsistency in this transliteration, but in no way does it affect the author's intended meaning. However, in a sustained passage in chapter 13 (page 119), I have preserved all diacritics in order to represent, particularly to an Arabist, the exact Arabic proper names whose English meaning follows them in parentheses.

This book won The University of Arkansas Press Award for Arabic Literature in Translation offered for the first time in 1993. As advertised, the award will be given annually for the best book-length translation of Arabic poetry and book-length translation of Arabic prose, and the winning book will be published by the University of Arkansas Press. I should like to thank the judges who considered my manuscript worthy of the award in June 1993. I should also like to thank Brian King, editor at the University of Arkansas Press, for his considerate help and sensitive reading of my translation, appreciative as he is of the many difficult decisions required to bring a work alive in a different language.

Issa J. Boullata

Author's Preface

I wanted at first to write a complete autobiography, especially because I had often asked the writers of my generation to write their memoirs and to record the experiences of change, growth, and conflict that gave flavor and meaning to their lives, to the lives of each of us, even to life as a whole in our age.

But I realized that if I intended to be accurate and expansive, I had to go back to a large number of documents, particularly letters I had written and others I had received over the years. And these amounted to thousands, in Arabic and English, to and from people in many countries. I discovered how difficult the project was because it was impossible to go back to most of these letters—since I had only a few in my possession. I realized that without these letters I would be obliged to depend on memory alone with all its gaps, its shaky uncertainties, and its confusions.

So I decided to write only about the first years of my life, beginning with my childhood as far back as memory could go, up to the time I ended my studies in England at the age of twenty-four and returned to Jerusalem full of ideas, feverishly obsessed by them, and torn between conflicting kinds of consciousness. Then I felt that my years of study at Exeter, Cambridge, and (for a short while) Oxford would alone require a special volume by themselves if I were to be true to myself and penetrating in writing about my experience. Therefore, I first thought I would begin by writing about my life up to the age of nineteen because two weeks or so after that I left Jerusalem in quest of a university education in England. That was the end of a phase and the beginning of another. At any rate, the first years of my life were full of personal experiences and events which had to be followed up and clarified, and writing about them would be exciting—though difficult—and would help me introduce the next phase more easily. But when I began to write about my first childhood memories, I discovered that I needed to summarize, delete, and neglect a lot of material. Otherwise, I would never finish. I realized again that the period which I had decided to write about was basically longer than necessary, for childhood is one thing and adolescence another. And although adolescence is essentially an extension of childhood experiences as far as one's growing vision of life is concerned, my adolescence was so rich and varied, and so full of pleasure, pain, love, and friendships that I could do it justice only in a separate volume. So I finally decided to be satisfied with the first twelve years of my life, or rather with seven or eight years of those, ending with my moving from Bethlehem to Jerusalem with my parents in 1932. This was, indeed, a decisive event in light of what followed.

When I began to review the events of my childhood, I discovered that during more than forty years of writing I had borrowed many of these events for my articles and short stories and especially my novels. Should I, then, deal with what I had written there as explication or fiction and rewrite them in a new context as purely autobiographical? No, I should not. Let me leave alone all the stories and narrative events that I had shaped from my childhood, and let scholars extract them and understand them as they would wish. But let me now deal with all that I had not used in my literary formulations, for it constituted no small quantity.

I remember I was once in a café in Jerusalem soon after the end of the Second World War in 1945. I met an attractive and intelligent lady named Heidi Lloyd, who said she was a sculptor and taught sculpture in Baghdad; her husband was a famous archeologist. At that time, I was president of the Arts Club and a lecturer in English literature at Rashidiyya College. I had written some poetry in English and had it published, and apparently she had read some of it. However, I was living under conditions of great hardship, and I did not want anyone to know.

When our coffee was served, she surprised me by saying, rather seductively, "Tell me about your life! I'm told you've lived, and still live, an exciting life."

I laughed and said, "An exciting life? I'm not the hero of all times, you know."

She said, "No, no . . . I don't mean that kind of life, but rather your physical life, your psychological and intellectual experience, your emotional relations. . . ."

In a flash, events from my childhood and adolescence and my years in England returned to me in wondrous speed, all mixed up.

I said, "If that's what you mean, I will tell you about my life, but not now. For the story is long, very long."

She asked, "Shall I, then, expect to read your autobiography one day?"

I replied, "I'm afraid you may have to wait too long. . . . And now, tell me about your sculpture and about Baghdad."

If in my younger days I thought the story was very long, what should I say now that it is forty years longer? The lady artist, whom I have never seen again, waited a long time indeed, even after I arrived in Baghdad three years later. Should I say she was the first person to sow the seed in my mind that I must one day speak about my life in one way or another?

I am not writing here a history of that era. There are those who are more knowledgeable, more worthy, and more skillful than I in going through the events of the 1920s and the early 1930s in Palestine. Nor am I here writing a history of my family, for that is another matter altogether, and I don't claim I have the ability to do it. I am also not writing a sociological analysis of a Palestinian town which was then small, with a population of no more than five thousand souls, if that, and whose schools did not go beyond primary education, most of which was dominated by churches, monasteries, and convents; today it is a town of some economic and political importance, with a population of almost eighty thousand; its schools are many, and it has a university from which dozens of students graduate every year.

What I have written is purely personal and purely childlike. My approach has been to focus on the self as its awareness increased, its perception grew, its sensibility deepened, and its bewilderment did not necessarily end. And lest I should slide into family history with all its ramifications (tempting as that may be), I have preferred to track the development of one single being who daily grew in consciousness, knowledge, and emotion and who lived in innocence and clung to it even as it gradually abandoned him. This developing being was, of course, part of his environment: he was part of the houses, trees, valleys, and hills; and he was part of the sun, the rain, the faces, and the voices which he lived surrounded by and in which he discovered values and morals, beauty and ugliness, joy and misery—one and all.

Perhaps I have made of the self and the environment, intentionally or unintentionally, two reciprocating subjects in each of which there was a reflection of the other, even a symbolic embodiment sometimes. And because both were constantly changing in time, I have tried to seize upon them, to pin them down, to capture them in a net of words lest they should be lost entirely.

However, the self and the environment were sometimes at odds. In a kind of madness, the self had to refuse to seek reflection in the environment and had to free itself from the latter's destructive effect till a day would come when it would control it and change it. Perhaps that is the story of one's adolescence or, at least, a part of it; this refusal to seek reflection is accompanied and later followed by a growing knowledge, a developing will, an increasing ability to analyze and explain, and a rising power to reconstruct and recreate through the imagination. It is, in fact, the story of lost innocence and the attempt to regain it.

One may feel that, after all these years and after all this great social transformation, the story of one's childhood actually comes without its full and real significance when it is separated from its later sequence, which is one's whole life. In the first place, childhood is not quite a single story, but many stories whose parts are often difficult to interlock, in spite of the recurrence of its characters, unless some fictional stratagem is used. And yet childhood urges the mind with repeated insistence to return to it. We find some of this insistence in night dreams, in which childhood appears each time in a new guise and with a different tension, and we find it unexpectedly in daydreams, where its presence is quite unlike mere recollections of memory.

Childhood stories, then, are stories of events which have become a blend of memory and dream, of existential intensity and poetic trance, a blend in which the rational and the irrational interpenetrate and intertwine. But it is a blend which always confirms its presence in some depth of the psyche which it is impossible to do justice to, however closely the mind may trace its parts and ramifications. Most writers of autobiography since the earliest of times and in the literatures of all nations actually tend to avoid this period or to neglect it altogether, perhaps because of its peculiar difficulty. If they ever concentrate on the events of their childhood, they are inclined to look at them with the eyes of a maturity which has come with age and the ability to explain and comment. So they try to clarify what happened to them in the past as an introduction to or a justification of their present. They try to forestall commentators and critics by commenting on their own experience and criticizing it. And since they don't always find much to comment on and criticize in connection with the years of their childhood, they seldom treat those years in more than one chapter or two. They hasten their pen in order to get to what they consider to be the more important stage of life, adolescence, especially as the psyche awakens to the beginnings of sexual feelings with their accelerating pleasures and pains. Then they concentrate on the stages that follow and give an account of the experiences of youth and maturity as evidence of what they have achieved—or have not achieved—in the fields of action or thought, or both.

Be that as it may, I have pursued a different path, perhaps keeping in mind Wordsworth's saying, "The Child is father of the Man." I have done so out of a deep desire to stress the beauty of that specific period of a person's life. It is beautiful probably because of its nearness to the source of being, especially if we believe, like Wordsworth again, that this source is rooted in Heaven with God. I have tried to go back and live that period again as a child, without any aching for analysis and without philosophizing about what happened or even commenting on it. I let myself go in this attempt as far as I could, but I was always obliged to select and delete, always aware of the writer's eternal problem—reconciling the fluidity of experience with the formalism of language. And there were certain events which I had to select, for they continued to impose themselves on my memory, to run in my blood with a sweetness I could not explain, with a beauty which grew in time, with a poetic fervor which burned more brightly as pain increased, and with the irony of the childlike love for every minute of that life, which may appear today to have been mostly cruel, unfair, and unacceptable.

In spite of the fact that the events of the next stage are necessarily much richer and more varied and complex, and although they also cry out to be captured in a net of words so that their outlines may thus be delineated in an intelligible form, childhood remains the source of a magic, constant and beyond explanation, the fountainhead of a radiance which cannot be defined. Both the magic and the radiance tempt us always to gaze at them and renew our wonder, as they provide the spirit with a freshness it is in need of whenever the stream of days piles up events on it and the passage of years loads it with burdens.

Jabra Ibrahim Jabra

Introduction

Whenever we wanted to move to a new house, the first thing we asked about was the well. Was there a well in the courtyard? Was it deep? Was it in good condition? Was its water good tasting? Or had the well not been emptied of its silt for years?

Wells were of as many kinds as houses. The mouth stones of the wells were also of many kinds. The mouth stone of a well is very much like a historical record of both the house and its well: with the passage of years, the bucket ropes that are lowered into the well and pulled up from it leave their tracks on the mouth stone. First they polish it smooth; then they cut grooves in it which become deeper and more numerous as the years pass by.

As for the wells, a few had an iron arch over them with a pulley in the middle, by which means ropes were lowered and raised as the pulley creaked; they were found only in big houses whose owners enjoyed a measure of luxury. Water was brought down into their wells through buried pipes, and some well-equipped wells might even have had pumps which allowed their people to dispense with buckets.

But the houses in which we resided had the primitive type of well: rainwater poured down from the spouts on the roof into the courtyard where it met with the water gathered there, then ran into a pit about one meter deep. This pit was near the well, and a little above the pit's bottom was a conduit leading into the inside of the well. The dirt carried by the rainwater sank to the bottom of the pit while the water, having thus been cleared a little, ran through the conduit leading to the well. The clearing process was not completed until many days later, when the sediments settled to the bottom of the well itself.

For this reason, a well had to be dredged every few years of its accumulated deposits. Wells such as these have preserved life for ages in the towns and villages of the mountain regions of Palestine where there is full dependence on winter rains in order to water the fields planted with wheat, barley, and millet and to water the hills and valleys abounding in olive, apricot, and almond trees and vines. The wells store rainwater for drinking and irrigation throughout the year. (As for orange groves, they are in the plains along the coast and have other means of irrigation.) Fortunate are the villages that have natural springs whose waters are usually crystal clear and ice cold.

Even though for drinking and cooking we scooped out water in a brass bowl from a large jar placed in one of the corners of the house, it was the water of the well that we drew in a bucket on days of great heat in order to enjoy a cold and refreshing drink. In winter, the water seemed to be less cold than that of the large jar. We also watered our small vegetable gardens from the well. When it was depleted, we had to beg water from the wells of our neighbors or buy it from the water carrier, who was one of the traditional characters of Bethlehem in those days, especially in certain parts of the town near Ayn al-Qanat, a fountain whose water ran from mountain springs that had been canalized centuries ago to make water available to many people who had no wells in their houses.

The water carrier used to carry water from this fountain on his back in a large black skin. When gasoline cans became available in the years of the First World War, first brought by the Ottoman army for its special uses, then by the petroleum companies afterward, the water carrier began fetching water in four-can loads on the back of his donkey, and he wore a black hide apron to protect himself from the constant dripping. We were often obliged to go to the fountain ourselves in order to fill our jars and cans amid noisy and screaming crowds of women and children; then we carried them home, however far, joyful for having obtained water.

The well!—how basic and vital it was! When we were obliged to live in a house that did not have a well in its courtyard, we really had a hard time of it.

The well of one's own life is that same primary well, with-out which living would not be possible. Experiences gather in it as water does in a well—to be turned to in times of thirst. Our life is but a chain of wells. We dig a new well in each phase and channel into it the water that gathers from the rains of the heaven and the flow of experiences—to go back to it when we are seized by thirst and when drought afflicts our land.

The first well is the well of childhood. It is that well in which are gathered our first experiences, the first sights and sounds, the first joys and sorrows, the first yearnings and fears which begin to rain on the child. These cause his understanding to increase and his awareness to grow under the stress of what he passes through every day: his agonies and his pleasures. Whenever he drinks from this well, he further adds to his understanding of these experiences, even as his thirst is being slaked. After many years, when a person draws water from this well, he never knows whether what will rise to him will be clear and cold or turbid and muddy. There may be much turbidity and muddiness and little clarity and coldness. And why not? That is what constitutes his life and his nourishment: it is the inevitable well. He cannot do without it. Every time he goes back to it, he actually drinks from a fountain of permanent abundance rising from the innermost depths of his humanity.

The First Well

1

First I became aware that my family called the place in which we lived the "khan." Then I became aware that all those who visited us described us as "the residents of the khan." Doubtless, the place must have been a khan—that is, a caravansary—sometime in the past. It was a large, deep room on the ground floor of an old building on the public road behind the mosque. Near it were many shops of all kinds, from that of the grocer to that of the maker of belts and donkey saddles. The room had no windows, and its iron door was big like that of a store. I could hardly move it because of its weight. Outside, near the door, there was a little toilet which must have been added after the house had been built during the long Ottoman period.

Between our door and the street, there was a small wooden gate used as an entrance to the building. It was likewise a later addition to the building, meant to separate it a little from the street. Whenever we crossed the high threshold of this entrance, we faced the door of the khan about six or seven steps away. To the left, in the open space, there was an uncovered stairway leading to the upper floor, which consisted of a single room with a green door. Frequently, I would see this door open whenever I went upstairs. Here lived a man with a short beard. He was always dressed in black, and I always saw him sitting at a table taking apart little instruments and putting them together again. He was Friar Yusuf, an expert at repairing watches and mechanical equipment. Past his room, the uncovered stairway led to a third floor in which was "the upper room."

The upper room was a large, rectangular room to which many men and women came on Sundays along with a number of boys wearing long white robes. They all sang as an old man with a long white beard wearing a brocaded blue garment stood in their midst. Now and then, his voice created a strange dissonance as he sang. Meanwhile, candles burnt everywhere.

My father explained to me that the room was a church, that it was the house of God, and that the old man was the Reverend Father Hanna, whose hand we should kiss whenever we met him. The scent of incense lingered on this floor all the days of the week. It had the kindness to come down to us residents of the khan whenever a suitable wind blew, and the air would then be redolent of its sweetness.

The khan was deep, damp, and dark except when the rays of the sun entered it in the morning, if the door was open. In one corner of it, my mother used to cook on a Primus kerosene stove which used to emit a sound of variable sharpness, depending on the size of its flame, and I felt it was singing. My mother, who used to sing with it sometimes, was skillful in pricking it with a special needle whenever it showed signs of refusing to burn as she wanted it to.

My father went out to work when I was still asleep. When my brother Yusuf and I woke up, we drank the tea which my grandmother usually prepared, and we ate some bread and olives with it. Then we went out to the street. Paved with flagstones, its cold surface used to bite our bare feet. Other boys like us would then come one after another, and we all went down together from the area behind the mosque toward the Square of Bab al-Dayr*, where cabs with horses stood and where perhaps two or three motorcars might be parked. People would then slowly flock to the place, get into the carriages and motorcars, or sit in the restaurants and cafés surrounding the square, while the sun would flood the place with light, with which the khan had nothing to compare. The terraces on the slopes and the distant mountains visible from the square would also be flooded with light and would begin to sparkle. The cold, which was the first thing we felt on going out, would then vanish.

One morning, after my brother had gone to school, I stayed

---

*I.e., the Square of the Monastery's Gate: this was the more common name for what was officially called the Square of the Manger, also known in English as the Square of the Church of the Nativity.

4

home with my mother and grandmother and watched my mother cook a dish she had promised me: *haytaliyya*, a rice-and-milk pudding. The milkwoman had knocked at our door, and my mother had bought a few pints of milk from her, which the milkwoman had poured into the cooking pot. This was an important event because my mother used to say she could not afford to buy milk except on special occasions and when absolutely necessary. I went upstairs to the upper floor to say good morning to Friar Yusuf, then to the church on the uppermost floor to look from the terrace at the boys down below playing in the street. I called out to them, and they called back to me, and by the time I came down to see how the *haytaliyya* was being cooked, the delicious, long-promised dish was ready.

My mother poured it into a flat metal tray, which she placed on the floor in the corner. She said, "Let's leave it for a couple of hours to cool. I'll give you some of it at noon, but we'll keep the rest for supper when your father will have returned from work because, like you, he likes *haytaliyya*."

My mother instructed me not to keep going in and out, and she bade me to be good while she went with my grandmother to the market to buy vegetables. She said, "If you go out, close the door well and don't permit anyone to come in."

No sooner was I alone than I looked at the white appetizing dish with burning desire. I stretched out my finger to it and tasted it. How delicious it was! But it was still hot, and my mother wanted it to be cold. "Well, let me go out to the street," I thought. And I took one more lick before I went out.

In the street, I met one of my friends near the door of the shop on the opposite side. I said to him, "You want to know something? My mother cooked *haytaliyya* for us today."

Walking behind the mosque, we met two other boys, and my friend said to them, "His mother has cooked *haytaliyya* today." A little while later, more of the neighborhood children gathered to play near the curve of the road. I said to them, "My mother has cooked *haytaliyya*."

One of them said, "Liar!"

I said, "You're a liar, yourself. Come and see."

Then I turned to the others and said, "Come on. Let's go to our home at the khan. We have *haytaliyya*."

They said, "But we're afraid of your mother."

I said, "My mother has gone out with my grandmother to the market."

We leapt and ran toward the khan. As usual, the outer gate was open; I let my friends in, and together we pushed open the big iron door of our house and entered. There were seven or eight of us.

In spite of the darkness, the rice-and-milk pudding on the floor was glowing like the sun. I dragged it to a spot near the door for more light, and I said, "Sit down."

They all sat down on the floor in a circle around the white dish, and I shouted at them, "Wait! Don't eat with your hands! We have spoons!"

Near the kerosene stove there was a plate containing a collection of different-sized spoons made of wood and aluminum. I distributed them, one by one, and found that I had no spoon. They began to eat, so I quickly took the ladle, crowded in among them, and ate with the rest of them.

In those wonderful moments as we were about to finish off the pudding, my mother entered with my grandmother behind her. She uttered a loud cry that shook the whole khan. The boys threw away their spoons and shot out of the open door like little devils and dashed off like the wind. Before my mother could lay her hands on me, I found myself running like a fury, my friends having scattered in all directions. I continued to run until I reached the entrance of the Church of the Nativity, alone and breathless.

I realized at that moment that my father had nothing left to eat in the evening upon his return from work. I also realized that I was the cause. I was afraid to return home.

I did not find any of my friends to play with. A short distance from the door of the Church of the Nativity, on one side of the square, there was a man drawing water with a bucket from the big mouth of a well. He poured the water into an oblong stone trough nearby. Three camels lowered their heads into it till their huge, thick lips almost touched its bottom. Sucking the water greedily, they displayed frightful yellow teeth. I stood there and watched their long curved necks, their enormous bodies, their extremely high legs, their great padded feet. I went around them slowly but was afraid to get too close to them. The man hardly poured a bucketful of water into the trough before the camels quaffed it in no time.

I left them and loitered about. I slowly drifted into the next street and stopped at the souvenir shops, looking at the mother-of-pearl rosaries and images and crosses in their windows and at the little olive-wood camels tied to one another in caravans.

After a while, my fear subsided or perhaps I forgot about it, and I began to feel hungry. I walked in the direction of our home. But at the door, I was afraid again of what my mother might do to me. I peeked in furtively and uttered, "Mom! Grandma!"

My brother came out to me, having returned from school. He laughed as he said, "Come in! You feed others with the spoon and reserve the ladle for yourself to eat with, don't you? Well, well! That's really great! Come on, hurry up!" He dragged me in to face my mother whose eyes glowed with anger.

Suddenly, I saw the anger in her eyes melt into a kind of laughter as she said, "You, devil! How dare you distribute our food to people? Do you think you are the son of Sulayman Jasir? You first eat and have enough, then feed other people."

She turned to my brother and said, "Yusuf, take this cooking pot and these two piasters. Run to the milkwoman's house and, if you find she still has any milk, buy six pints and come back quickly so that I may cook another dish of *haytaliyya* for your father. . . . As for this your brother, I swear by God he will not taste it! Take him with you, too. I don't want to see his face!"

In the evening, my mother gave up her threat. In an affected, commanding tone she shouted, "Come on! Sit down with your father and brother. Do you want the ladle to eat with or is the spoon good enough for you?"

Early the next morning, my father took me upstairs to the church with my brother. He made me stand in one of the two lines of choir boys. Although I did not know what they sang in Syriac, I enjoyed what I heard, and I tried to raise my voice with them as they sang. I watched the boy who carried the censer as he drew it near Father Hanna. With a little spoon, the priest would take some incense from a copper bowl in the boy's hand and feed it to the embers in the censer over which he made the sign of the cross. The boy would then go around in the church, through the congregation, shaking the censer rhythmically, as it gave out clouds of fragrance.

I wished I could carry a censer like him to cense the people, the house, the stairs, and all the inhabitants of the neighborhood and their homes. My father had said that angels rose with the clouds of incense and brought down God's blessings upon all those who smelled the lovely scent. How I wished I could see those angels!

Seeing the angels remained an unfulfilled desire, making me sometimes imagine I saw them in some ghostly form— creatures that were midway between birds and women. I imagined I could play with them and invite them to a dish of rice-and-milk pudding. We would be able to eat as we liked because my mother would not see the angels, and perhaps she would not see me, either, because I was in their company.

I used to hear stories about devils also: they were black and had sharp horns; they emitted fire from their mouths and cracked their long tails. But they liked neither the sweetness of incense nor the music of beautiful hymns. I did not think they liked to be friends with children or eat rice-and-milk pudding, either. And thank God for that because I never wanted to see them. If a devil ever appeared to me, I would close our iron door smack in his face and let him knock at it with his tail until he had his fill!

My brother used to go to the German school at Madbasa. My mother said to him one day, "Take your brother with you; I want to take care of my chores."

When my brother took me to school, the principal gave me a quick look, shook his head, and asked Yusuf, "How old is this brother of yours?"

"Five years," my brother said.

"Take him back home," the principal said. "And let him come to us again after one year."

My mother was angry when my brother brought me home, and she immediately took me to the Greek Orthodox school, which was nearer to our home than the German school. She met the teacher, and he said to her, "He's welcome. Leave him with us and go in peace. Or rather bring him tomorrow morning before eight o'clock."

But we were all occupied on the next day with moving to another house. It was a place we reached by going up many stairs. I became aware that we called our new home by a name new to me: *al-khashashi* (the huts).

At school I saw the students writing. Each of them took his lead pencil, opened his copybook, and wrote on the ruled white paper. They raised their heads and looked beyond the teacher's head to the board, which was made of pieces of wood in a square frame, propped on a tripod. It had been painted black at one time, but it was almost white now because, though constantly erased, it retained accumulated chalk. Moreover, its pieces of wood were now falling apart. The teacher had written a few letters on this board, and the boys were writing. Each of them put out his tongue automatically, wet the point of the pen on the tip of his tongue, and wrote. Each had a small eraser with the picture of an elephant on it, and with it he erased errors. When the pencil tip broke, he sharpened it with a sharpener before he dipped the sharp, black tip in his saliva again, looked at the board, and wrote.

That was my first day, or one of my first days, at the Greek Orthodox school situated behind the Church of the Nativity. I said to the teacher as I sat on a long bench with four or five other children like me, "Shall I also write, sir?"

He asked, "Have you brought your copybook and pencil with you?"

"No," I replied.

"How can you write, then?" he asked.

I answered, "In the copybook of one of the boys who have copybooks."

The boys laughed. Even the teacher laughed, and he said, "No, my boy. Bring your own copybook and pencil tomorrow, and then you can write."

A short while later, the teacher rang a bell. We went out to the playground. There was a large, slanting pine tree which almost divided the small yard into two parts. I jumped onto the bent trunk and climbed up to the highest branches. A group of other boys followed me. We had hardly played at all when the teacher rang the bell again. We returned to the classroom. There were at least fifty boys of different ages. Most of the boys seemed to me older than I was: they were ten, twelve, and some of them perhaps fifteen years old. And I was only five, and I was barefooted. Most of us were barefooted, but some of the older boys wore large boots left to their parents by the Ottoman army.

Before noon we went home for the lunch hour. I went running and found my grandmother in the garden looking at the shadow cast by the almond tree on the wall of the house. She asked, "Why have you come back before time?"

"But it is lunch hour."

"No, my dear. The shadow has not yet reached this stone," she said, pointing to a protruding stone in the wall. "Do you think I don't know when noon is?"

"I don't know. The teacher let us out and said to return at one o'clock."

My grandmother then called out, "Maryam, prepare lunch. Your son is back!"

I had a special relationship with my grandmother behind my mother's back. She knew that my mother was quick tempered and that, if I did anything my mother did not approve of, I would be given a sound beating. So she covered up for me.

I approached her. Her dress was long, almost reaching the ground. I touched it, and she said, "What's the matter, now? Have you something to say? Have you done something wrong?"

Looking at her honey-colored eyes, I said, "Grandma, I want to buy a copybook and a pencil."

"A copybook and a pencil! Why?"

"In order to write."

"Tell your mother that. Ask her what you want or wait till your father returns in the evening."

When I entered the house, my mother was looking into the cooking pot and stirring its contents. She said, "Welcome to the schoolboy!"

"Mother," I said, "the teacher says I should take a copybook and a pencil with me to school."

"Really? And how am I to get you a copybook and a pencil?"

"The copybook and the pencil cost half a piaster. That's what the boys say."

"And who says I have half a piaster? Come, sit down and eat, and forget the copybook and the pencil. Half a piaster, indeed! And before you eat, take out some grass to the two sheep."

I took out some of the grass we collected in a large bag when we went out to the fields so that we did not have to take the two sheep out to pasture every day. I carried it to the two white sheep tied in the hut. They were chewing their cuds after having rolled in the dirt on the ground. As soon as they saw me, they rose. I gave them some grass, and they began to munch it eagerly as I rubbed their backs with my hand.

My mother poured out the food into a large dish placed on the floor, and we sat around it. "Listen! The noon hour is striking now!" she said as the steeples of the monasteries all over town started to ring their bells announcing midday, their sounds blending in the air, clear and joyful.

After lunch, I returned to school, and we played until the teacher rang his bell. We entered the classroom. No pupil wrote anything this time, but the teacher wrote letters of the Arabic alphabet on the board and asked a group of us to repeat them after he read them aloud.

"Alif."

And we shouted, "Alif."

"Ba'."

"Ba'."

"Ta'."

"Ta'."

"Alif Ba'."

"Alif Ba'."

When we were sent out later in the afternoon, two of my friends and I began to repeat and sing rhythmically, "Alif Ba' bubini, half a loaf and zucchini." We passed by the shop of Hanna Tabash, displaying copybooks, pencils, and erasers in the window. I entered and said to the salesman, "I want a pencil and a copybook."

"Do you have half a piaster?"

"No."

"Go, then, and bring half a piaster, and I will give you the best pencil and the best copybook."

I returned home and found my grandmother in the garden taking down the laundry from the clothesline. I looked at her with hopeful eyes. She understood me immediately, and without saying a word, she put her hand in her bosom, took out a knotted handkerchief, and untied two knots. When the handkerchief was opened, there were four or five coins in it. She picked a half-piaster coin, and she said, "Here. Don't tell your mother. And show me your heels, gallop away!"

I ran, galloping away to the shop of Tabash. I handed the shopkeeper the dear coin, and he gave me a copybook and a pencil. I asked him to sharpen the pencil for me, so he did and said, "If you don't have a sharpener, that's not necessary. Sharpen the pencil with a razor blade."

I rushed back home carrying what I had just bought. My mother was not at home, and my grandmother was occupied with family chores as usual. Near the door of our house, there was a long stone bench, so I lay down on my stomach, opened my copybook at the first page, and took the new, sharpened pencil to write. I wet its sharp point on the tip of my tongue.

But what would I write? I tried to remember the letters which the teacher had written on the board that morning and in the afternoon. The Alif *(A)* was easy. Its shape in Arabic, as the teacher said, was like that of a stick. The Ba' *(B)* was a stick lying down with upturned edges. So I wrote *A A A A* then *B B B,* and the line was full. I started another line, and yet another. But I found that my lines were sloping down in spite of all my efforts. I changed the position of the copybook in front of me, and I wrote, but the lines continued to slope downwards from right to left. The page was filled with sloping lines. I filled another, then another. Suddenly, the pencil tip broke, and I stopped.

That evening, my copybook was the family's spectacle. My father said, "Well done!" Yusuf said, "Your lines are running downhill—perhaps to drink?" My mother said, "Write correctly and take care of the copybook. And don't you lose the pencil. Do you hear me?" My grandmother winked at me, in full understanding.

Next morning, I took my "tools" to school. I said to the teacher, "I've brought my copybook and pencil."

He said, "Fine. Sit down in your place and write."

The teacher sharpened my pencil, I borrowed an eraser, and I began writing. But the boys next to me were not writing because they had no copybooks. They laughed and fidgeted. They continuously indulged in horseplay with their bare feet. One of them pushed another and kicked him under the bench. Another kicked my foot, causing my pencil to make a long scratch on the page in front of me.

At lunch my mother asked me, "Has the teacher seen your copybook?"

I said, "Yes, indeed."

When I tried to show her what I had written, she said, "How can I read it when I don't know how to read?"

In the afternoon, we did not write anything. The teacher was sleepy. He sat at his table, asked an older boy to stand up in front, and said to him, "Elias, you are the prefect today. Whoever talks or laughs or even breathes—write me his name on the board. . . . And you, boys of the first and the second classes,

13

open your reading books to page five and read. But, no noise! And you there, sitting at the back, put your folded arms on the desks thus, rest your heads on them, and sleep. And don't move, do you understand?"

He then closed his eyes. His head soon fell on his chest, and he was sound asleep.

We buried our faces in our folded arms, as the teacher had instructed us. But who of us, devils that we were, could sleep? With our heads on the desks, we spent an hour chattering and laughing. When we raised our heads, Elias had written three or four names on the board. He had also put a cross next to one of them. Suddenly, the teacher gave a mighty snore and raised his head immediately afterward. His terrifying eyes roved about the boys' faces. Then he slowly turned his head toward the board and saw the names. He called out the first of them, "Jiryis! Come here."

Jiryis came out from among his companions and walked with fear toward the teacher, "I swear by God, sir, I did not speak and did not laugh."

Taking his long ruler, the teacher said, "Open your hand!"

"By God, sir. . . ."

"Open your hand. And no nonsense!"

The boy opened his hand, and the teacher struck him once on his palm with the ruler.

The teacher did likewise to the second person named. As for the person whose name was marked with a cross, the teacher hit him twice. Then the bell rang, and we were dismissed.

My classmate next to me on the bench was called Abdu. He accompanied me on my way back and convinced me to go with him to his home by saying, "Do you know how to make a cracker? This copybook has sixteen leaves, and from every two you can make one cracker."

His mother was preoccupied with her sewing when we sat on the floor in one corner of their house. Abdu took the copybook from my hand, but I took it back. He said, "Only one cracker then, that's all." I handed him the copybook. He opened it and removed the center page; then he folded it in a special way while I watched him. He placed it under his armpit and pressed it with his arm. He then pulled it out quickly and gave it a violent shake. It gave out a wonderful, explosive sound. He folded it again and repeated the act. Again it cracked. Wonderful!

"Shall I make you one, too?" he asked.

"I'll make my own," I answered.

I removed another page from the copybook and made a cracker—and it snapped! Then we made another and yet another, until we came to the end of the copybook. Abdu's mother was giving us little attention, but from time to time, she said, "Stop that noise, you boys!"

We went out to the street, snapping and cracking. Our pockets were an arsenal of crackers. We saw friends of ours and distributed the crackers to them. We all began to snap again and again, till the sun set and the crackers were all torn.

I hastened back home.

My grandmother asked, "Where is the copybook?"

"The teacher took it," I replied.

My mother asked, "Where is the copybook?"

"The teacher took it," I said.

"Why? To have fun looking at it?"

"To keep it in his drawer lest it should be lost."

When my father returned from his work, he asked me, "Where is the copybook?"

I said, "It's with the teacher."

My brother Yusuf asked me the same question at supper, and I gave him the same answer.

That night, I slept, thinking of the crackers. I was sorry I had not kept at least one to crack at school. But I was also afraid a little. How would I be able to buy another copybook?

On the next day, I went to school. I had nothing but the pencil, so I doodled with it on the top of the desk. Whenever its tip broke, I sharpened it with the help of one of the other boys until it was almost half gone.

At home I was showered again with the same question, "Where is the copybook?" And I answered, "With the teacher."

In the morning of the third day, when the bell rang, Abdu pulled me by the arm. I said, "What kind of school is this? Bells, bells! Always bells!"

He said, "Let's skip school, man. Will you come with me?"

I said, "Let's go."

We went running out of the playground gate toward Manger Square. There were cars parked there from which tall, blond, elderly men and women got out carrying cameras. They spoke to us in a language we did not understand, so they gestured to us to stand in front of them with the Church of the Nativity in the background, so that they might take our picture.

Noon hour struck suddenly. I ran home and my grandmother welcomed me, the schoolboy, and she said, "I cooked the best lentil soup for you today. Fetch an onion, smash it, and sprinkle some salt on it."

Onions whet one's appetite for lentil soup, and lentil soup whets one's appetite for more onions. So I ate until I was full, then I lay down on my back. My mother chided me, "Get up, get up! Go to your school. Have you forgotten? And tell the teacher to give you back your copybook."

My grandmother said to her, "Take it easy. Let the boy rest a little."

My mother said, "By God, you have spoiled him!"

I went to Abdu's home.

For several days, he and I went down the valley or loitered around Manger Square. When it was time for schoolchildren to be dismissed, we returned home in order to make our parents believe we continued to go regularly to school.

Hardly had four or five days passed, when my mother confronted me at noon time, standing at the garden gate waiting for me. When I pushed open the gate, she seized me by the ear and pulled with mighty strength saying, "Where is the copybook?"

"Mother, I told you. It's with the teacher."

"With the teacher? You liar!"

She slapped my cheek. "I saw Abdu's mother this morning, and she told me everything." She slapped my other cheek, "You've filled the street of Ras Iftays with crackers. You liar!

You thief! And you made fools of us too! By God, you shall never see school again!"

In spite of my grandmother's protection, I was given a first-class thrashing. All my grandmother could do was to thrust a piece of bread and a tomato in my hand as I wept in the garden, and she pushed me out and let me escape. I went out and sat on the steps leading down to the street. I ate my miserable lunch, the salty tears burning my eyes, and my mother's pinching still stinging my cheeks and thighs.

That evening, my father decided to send me to the Syriac Catholic school where he knew the teacher, for he was our neighbor. My father thought he would thus be able to know if I was regularly present at school and whether I was actually learning the alphabet like a decent human being.

 3

Our house consisted of a small room built of rough stones. Attached to it was a terraced green plot in which grew two pomegranate trees, an almond tree or two, and a large fig tree. Nearby was "the hut," also built of rough stones, which had a flagstoned courtyard, in the midst of which was the well. This courtyard was connected with another terraced green plot surrounded by pomegranate trees. A passageway separated the two green plots and ran between our dwelling and the hut where the sheep and chickens were kept. Branches of an old vine arched over a part of this passageway, which stretched from an old gate whose rusted tin panels merged with time-worn wood.

Our one-room house and our hut were both roughly roofed over with logs, and the trunks and branches were clearly visible in the low ceilings. Extending from wall to wall, they were closely woven together and were covered with a thick layer of mud and soil. One of our tasks from time to time, especially before winter arrived, was to pack down the roof with a heavy stone roller. This, of course, did not prevent the ceiling from leaking or water from seeping in when it rained, but it did diminish the damage and kept it contained primarily in the corners. I often lay on my back on the earthen floor of the room or on the straw mat and watched the rats that nestled in the crevices of the ceiling logs. They would fight until one rat defeated another and knocked him to the ground. Our cat, Fulla, would pounce on the victim, picking him up neatly and carrying him carefully between her teeth to the garden, where she would put an end to him in her own feline way. In spite of her apparent gentle nature and her pleasant name, Fulla revealed the ferocity of a tigress when confronting her prey. I often saw her fix mice with a look that froze them with fear; then she ate them. But one day she was nearly beaten by a rat almost as big as she was. He raised his front foot and clawed at her snout while in a frenzied battle with her. She finally managed to at least make him flee and vanish from her sight.

Behind our house, walls and other houses rose in tiers to the top of the mountain, on whose slope the town had been built many ages ago. In front of our house and beyond the entrance, an alley led to a steep flight of stairs descending to the main road known as Ras Iftays, or Star Street as it was later called. In order to reach the alley of our house from the main road, we climbed the irregular stone stairs, polished by many footsteps over the years. The stairway was not very wide. At the right of its bottom step was a magnificent house of regular, smoothly chiseled stones, with an iron gate that had once, a long time ago, been painted white. At the left of the bottom step was a high wall with a manger at its foot. A white donkey was tied in this manger, and whenever it stood across the stairway entrance with its head in the manger and its hind part toward the house, it occupied more than half of the entrance. The donkey belonged to the Greek doctor who lived in the house. I don't think anyone called this Greek doctor by his name or even knew what it was. He was the most reputable doctor in town, and everybody simply called him by the only name they respected: the Greek doctor. His donkey enjoyed a class distinction among the many donkeys in town because its aristocratic white color stood out from the poor, grayish color of all the other donkeys. We used to see the Greek doctor riding his donkey, with his medical bag in the donkey's red saddlebag. Haughtily, he would urge the animal on with a short bamboo cane as he went on his rounds. He was a short fat man. He was clean shaven, and gray hair was beginning to mix with the black at his temples. He wore a hat and never smiled at anyone or anything.

No friendly relations ever arose between the doctor—or his donkey—and me. Still, one of my earliest experiences in this neighborhood was with this respected donkey when I was five years old. I wanted to climb the stairs to go home, but the donkey stood in the way, almost blocking the entrance with its body. It had apparently finished eating its fodder, and its dung and straw filled the two or three bottom steps. I avoided the dung as best I could and headed toward the narrow opening left for the passersby next to the donkey's rear end. The donkey was whisking away the flies and the gadflies with its tail. I don't think that I lingered to look at its tail and the insects when I passed, although I might have perhaps raised my hand in the direction of the tail to protect myself from its switching. Before I knew it, the donkey had given me a formidable double kick with its hind legs, giving my shoulder and chest such a powerful blow that I screamed as I sped by and climbed the upper steps, weeping and terrified. It was a painful lesson early in my life that taught me never to get too close to donkeys, and to be exceedingly wary if I had to approach them and their likes.

Once, my mother was very ill for a couple of days and unable to move around. I didn't know what exactly the matter was with her when I saw her unable to get off her mattress spread out on the floor. She was writhing with pain and moaning. My grandmother asked me to go down the stairway to the Greek doctor's house before he went out on his rounds and to ask that he come to our house to treat my mother. Had I not realized that the matter was serious, I would not have risked entering the doctor's house when his donkey was tied to the manger one or two steps away from the door. I summoned my courage and went into the house. The doctor was in the hall, preparing to go out. Before I had time to say "good morning," as my grandmother had instructed me, he frowned and asked, "What are you doing here, boy?"

"My mother is sick, doctor," I stammered.

"And who is your mother?"

"My mother? Er, she's Umm Yusuf, the wife of Hajj Ibrahim."

"Do you want me to visit her? Where do you live?"

I don't remember his words exactly, for, in the first place, I did not understand many of them because of his Greek accent. But I must have explained what I wanted, for he accompanied me to the top of the stairway and to our house. He entered, and my grandmother received him by pulling out a pillow from a recess and placing it on the mat for him to sit on. The visit was not long: he examined my mother in one way or another, reassured her, then wrote a prescription which he gave to my grandmother. He stood up and asked to be paid a five-piaster fee for his visit. "Five piasters!" my mother said in surprise, in spite of her pain. "What have you done, doctor, to charge five piasters? My husband works from daybreak till sunset for five piasters."

I felt he was asking the impossible of us.

The doctor was displeased, but he said, "All right, give me two or three piasters."

My mother thrust her hand under her pillow, pulled out one shilling (one five-piaster coin), and gave it to him, proudly saying, "No, no. Here you are. Thank you very much."

The doctor took the shilling and dropped it in the small pocket of his waistcoat. I noticed the fine chain stretching from one of the buttons to the opposite pocket: he pulled it carefully and took out a golden watch, which he opened to check the time. Then he closed the shining cover with a smart tap of his finger and returned the watch to his pocket. Picking up his bag, he went out.

My mother said, "Now, quick, run to your school, darling."

I had enrolled in a new school, and my mother had made me a cloth bag which I carried by a strap across my shoulder and in which I put my school things. In addition to my new copybook, I now had a reader and a calligraphy copybook. I took the bag and rushed in the direction of the New Road, where the school stood next to a newly built church. The school consisted of one large room furnished with long desks.

When I entered the school, Teacher Samuel stopped me. He addressed me in classical Arabic, "Why are you late, boy?"

I said, "I took the Greek doctor home to see my mother."

"Why?" he asked. "Is she ailing?"

I said, "She has a bellyache, teacher."

The boys laughed as though I had told them a joke. The teacher said, enunciating his words, "Say she is sick . . . well, may God heal her. Sit down in your place."

Whenever Teacher Samuel spoke, my friends and I wondered at the strange words he uttered. Many of them we did not quite understand, though we guessed their meaning—sometimes. He taught us the alphabet in one or two weeks; then he gave us a reading book and rushed us through its pages, considering them not worthy of lengthy study. *Ras, rus / Dar, dur*—we read the words and copied them from the book. He took our copybooks, corrected them in beautiful red ink, and returned them to us, saying, "Scrawls of chickens, that's what your handwriting is!"

In between reading and writing lessons, he used to tell us stories by way of religious instruction. He told us how God made some clay and from it created a man He called Adam. And while Adam was sleeping under one of the trees of Paradise, God took a rib from his chest and from it created a woman that He called Eve. The teacher also told us a sad story about how the criminal Cain killed his good brother Abel. As I imagined God making clay as the construction workers did in Bethlehem, I also imagined Cain's dreadful face, marked on the forehead with the disgrace of God's curse, as the criminal wandered aimlessly in wilderness and city. I would look at people's faces in the streets and at their foreheads, wondering whether Cain was one of them.

When I sat in my place that morning, the teacher was telling the story of the Flood and Noah's ark, which Noah filled with birds and animals. The Greek doctor's donkey crossed my mind, and I wished that Noah had left the donkey's forefather to the waters of the Flood, for he would have saved us from that obdurate donkey who blocked our way and threatened passersby with double kicks of his fearful hooves.

That afternoon, toward the end of classes, I needed to urinate badly. I raised my hand and said to the teacher, "May I go out, teacher?"

He said, "We'll all go out in a few moments."

My neighbor Salim suddenly raised his hand and said, "Teacher, teacher, I must go out!"

The teacher told him off, "In a moment, wait now. We'll all go out after reciting Hail Mary." Then he shouted, "Stand up!"

We all stood up; I shifted my weight from one foot to the other, trying to control my bladder as best I could. I noticed that my neighbor's predicament was no less distressing than mine. The teacher continued, "Let us pray."

We began praying: "Hail Mary, full of grace. The Lord is with thee. Blessed art thou amongst women. . . ."

We had hardly come to the end of the prayer when we saw a furtive stream gently flowing under the seats toward the teacher. Salim had "done it." He could not control himself. The boys burst out laughing, "Salim pissed in his pants; he pissed in his pants!"

The teacher screamed at us, "Get out, you impolite, uncivil boys!"

Had we been delayed one minute longer, I would have committed the same crime as my neighbor. I shot like a bullet toward the backyard and emptied my bladder under a large fig tree while the boys were still hooting hilariously. When I returned to them, Salim was crying, his short pants and legs scandalously wet.

On our way back home, I saw the Greek doctor bustling along on his donkey. He passed by us, and I expected him to ask me something or to say a word that showed he recognized me. But he went on his way hurriedly, knocking his white donkey with his knees, urging it with a cluck of his tongue, his hat perched on his head like some strange bird. I wondered, Was my mother better? Was she up and about? Or was she still in bed? And I hurried home before the doctor returned and tied his accursed beast at the entrance of the stairway.

4

My brother Yusuf was four years older than I. He and his friends appeared to me to belong to a world other than mine—the world of adults. Whenever he said anything, I was all ears, and I felt he was admitting me into his world. He, too, went to school, but he hung out with friends who were his age or older. After he left home in the morning, I sometimes did not see him again until he returned home—and that might not be until evening.

In addition to Arabic books, he had an English book on each page of which was an color illustration or a line drawing. I often sat by him, and he showed me the pictures and boasted of his ability to read the English words under each, which I could not because I had yet to learn English.

One evening, he brought me a cardboard box and said, "Do you know what this box is? It is the 'Box of the World.' Come and look."

In the middle, there was a round opening with a magnifying lens we called "the crystal." I placed my right eye to it and closed my left. From the top of the box, my brother began to turn one of two spindles; and a paper tape, on which all kinds of pictures were stuck, began to move. As the spindles turned, the pictures inside the box passed one after the other before the lens: because they were enlarged and distorted, they acquired a strange magic.

My brother's box fascinated me, and I wished that he would leave it at home for me and permit me to take it to my friends to show it to them. But he hid it away, and I could not find it.

One afternoon, while Abdu and I were playing in the

Square of the Church of the Nativity, we saw the real Box of the World. It was a large, blue, wooden box, in the middle of which were three big lenses. Its owner placed it on a movable stand and put mirrors and oleographs of women, horsemen, and horses on its top. He shouted, "Come and look! See the wonders of all time!" Abdu and I longed to go and look, but where could we come by the dear fee of half a piaster?

We stood near the box and looked in wonder at its form and decoration until two or three men came up. The owner sat them on boxes in front of the glass openings. They placed their eyes close to the lenses, and he began to turn the spindle from above and to sing in rhyming words about Antar and Abla, al-Zir Salim, Abu Zayd, Kawkab al-Sharq, and Munira al-Mahdiyya. Listening and gazing at the box which contained all those wonders, we ate our hearts out. The boys gathered around, all looking in anguish. Other people came and sat in front of the lenses and peeped, and others after them. Suddenly, my friend took out a sesame cake from inside his shirt and said to the showman, "Will you let me and my friend look if I give you this cake?"

The man said, "You and your friend for this measly piece?"

"Yes, me and my friend," he answered.

The man took the cake and bit off a morsel of it, saying as he chewed, "Okay, come. You sit here, and you sit there."

Actually, only one client remained, and so he made us sit with him. He then began to recite his rhyming commentary, as the brightly colored pictures passed in succession behind the magic lens: hunters with their horses and dogs, kings on their thrones, soldiers being shot and killed, half-naked women. There was hardly any connection between the pictures and his narration, but the suggestions were great. And the show ended all too soon.

That evening, when he returned from work, my father brought home an old tire. My mother brought the washbasin, and when she washed his feet, I noticed how large they were and how they seemed to be made of rock. My father then washed his face and dried it. He brought the toolbox, containing a hammer, an anvil, pincers, strange sharp knives, a whetstone whose black color shone brightly with the oil on it, nails of all kinds, chisels, and rolls of waxed threads and wires. He took the car tire and, using one of the knives, laboriously cut off two pieces. He then put his right foot in the curvature of one piece and made a mark with the knife at the toes. He took his foot off and cut the piece to the right length. He did the same with the other piece, while I watched him closely.

With much effort, he pierced holes along the sides of each piece and put a thin rope through them, first in one side and then in the other. Meanwhile, my mother was going to and fro in her wooden clogs, and occasionally out into the courtyard to assure herself that the pot was boiling on the fire, all the while calling to me and my brother, "Bring me some firewood! Draw a bucket of water from the well! Fill the large water jar. . . ."

My father finished what he was doing, and I saw him push his feet into the curved pieces of tire, tying them tightly around his ankles. He then said, proud of what he had made, "You see, Maryam? The best sandals!"

I did not like the sight of these "sandals" and said, "Dad, why don't you buy a pair of shoes from the shoemaker?"

He said, "When you grow older, you'll understand. Do you know how much the shoemaker will charge for a pair of shoes? Twenty piasters! If he is charitable, he may charge fifteen. . . . My old shoes are beginning to wear out because of use. I will therefore keep them for Sundays. So, what do you think now, Mister?"

He took his feet out of the sandals and said, "Let's have supper. Tonight I have a new story to tell you, the story of Ashrawiyya."

I asked my brother, "Where is the Box of the World?"

"I returned it to its owners," he laughingly replied.

"At the Church Square today," I said, "I looked in the large Box of the World. It's fantastic!"

"If I had pictures to use," he said, "I would make you a most wonderful box."

My father interrupted, "What's the matter with you, boys? Aren't we going to tell a story tonight?"

We all said, "Of course, of course we are, Father."

The following day was a Sunday. On Sundays we didn't go to school, and everybody went to church. As for me, I headed toward Abdu's house and brought him back home with me. He had a cardboard shoe box his father had come by two days earlier, and we spent that morning preparing the materials for our project: newspaper for the ribbon, a bottle of glue, a piece of glass for "the crystal," and two sticks we brought from the heap of firewood which my mother and grandmother collected.

Two or three hours later, everything was ready—except for the pictures. Abdu went home in haste and brought back three or four faded family photographs which did not appeal to me very much. At that moment, I remembered my brother's English book. My brother was away with his friends at Ras Iftays or in the playground of Father Anthony's Monastery. I took out the book from his school bag, and when my friend saw it, he could not believe his eyes. I got my mother's scissors while she was too preoccupied to know what we were busy with in the garden, and we started to cut the pictures out, leaf by leaf, and to stick them on the ribbon, until nothing remained of the book but shreds. Abdu suggested that we burn the shreds to get rid of the evidence, and that was exactly what we did. We went out to the alley and set them on fire. In two minutes, we concealed all traces of our theft.

We took the Box of the World to our friends to show it to them and arouse their wonder and jealousy. We called it the "Cinema" and shouted: "Free Cinema! No charge!"

We soon regretted our generosity. All the neighborhood boys gathered and began snatching the Cinema from one another. The box was battered, and it collapsed in their hands. The glass piece dropped out of its place, the cover fell off, and nothing remained but the picture ribbon. When I tried to save it, someone pulled one end of it and it tore. Another pulled the other end, tearing it again. Finally, Abdu and I sat on the threshold of one of the closed shops, with the last remains of our wrecked project. Abdu then left for his home, and I was overwhelmed by a feeling of defeat, and I wept.

My misery was complete when my brother came along in the company of his friends as the sun was setting, and he saw me huddled in the corner of the entrance of the closed shop. "Come on, let's go home," he said merrily.

Although I tried to hide my tears, my brother Yusuf realized how miserable I was. "Are you crying?" he asked. "Who beat you? Just tell me who did, and I'll break his head."

I pointed to the torn pictures, scattered at my feet, and I said, "The Box of the World—they tore it to pieces."

He picked up some shreds, then threw them away. He helped me up saying, "Are you crying for this? I'll make you a thousand boxes instead. . . . Come."

But when I thought of what he would do to me when he discovered what I had done to his book, I began to cry again as I walked with him. All of a sudden he asked me, "Where did you manage to get the pictures?"

Trusting God with my fate, I said, "From your English book."

"What?" he shouted. "What did you say?"

"From your English book," I repeated.

He stopped walking, and I expected him to slap me. He was strong and was known among his friends as always being ready to beat up those who attacked him, whether young or old.

He looked me in the face, holding me by the shoulders. I gasped as I wept, but he said, "Quiet! Damn the book! . . . Tomorrow I'll get another one. But keep quiet, just keep quiet!"

He looked to left and right, and said proudly, "I don't want anyone ever to see you crying. Ever! Understand?"

He dragged me by the hand as we went running back home.

5

One particularly good thing about that house of ours which we called *al-khashashi* was that it had two terraced plots with several pomegranate and almond trees, a large fig tree, and a vine that in vain tried to spread over the passageway leading to the house. In these terraced plots, I read my first words and wrote my first letters of the alphabet. In them, I was surprised to see my mother, on a cold afternoon, wrap her shoulders with a blanket and accompany my father to the hospital of the Sisters of Charity. Two or three days later, when she returned home with a swaddled little baby in her arms, I asked her where she brought him from. Laughingly, she said, "From the hospital, my darling." That baby was my brother Issa who was six years younger than I and who, I continued to believe for a long time afterward, was a gift from the hospital!

In these terraced plots, I sang my first songs and slowly began to understand some of their meanings. My brother Yusuf was my teacher most of the time, in addition to our only teacher at the Syriac Orthodox School, Teacher Jiryis. I also began to be aware of the differences in people's characters and behaviors, and I wondered why they did not obey the instructions of their parents and the sermons of their priests and monks.

I gathered a group of my friends in these plots in order to stage a play like those we often saw at Father Anthony's Monastery. Later, we performed many plays, and they all had to end in a fight which I would insist on continuing until the others finally admitted I was the winner. As a result of this insistence, a little tragedy left its scar on my face, which is visible until this day. In one of those final fights, a number of boys banded together against me, and among them were two brothers well known for biting. When I resisted and did not admit defeat, the acting turned into real fighting; I was unaware that the brothers had become angry. One of the them bit my cheek and removed part of my skin and flesh, while the other sunk his teeth into my breast and nearly tore out my nipple. They did not leave me until they saw blood flowing over my face and their clothes and I was screaming and crying.

In that house of ours, I became conscious for the first time of the harshness and terror of nature. As I woke up on a severely cold day, I found that my father had left his bed where I usually sought warmth, being unable to sleep anywhere but near him. He, my mother, grandmother, and brother were trying to remove a mound of snow from the doorway. It had been snowing all night, and when my father opened the door to check on the weather outside, drifts of snow that had piled up at the door slid inside. So we all set about scooping the snow outside with our hands or with any available utensil. But where could we throw it, when everywhere the snow was more than knee deep?

It seems my father had expected this snowstorm and had made a shovel from a rod, at one end of which he had fixed a triangle of sticks. With this contraption, he shoveled the piles of snow away from the door, and we helped him to open a passageway out. Meanwhile, he kept repeating as he looked anxiously at the ceiling logs, "I am afraid the ceiling might cave in. I must go up to the roof before the snow makes it collapse on us." I thought the whole house might collapse on us before my father could save the situation.

We wanted to go out in the snow with my father, but he forbade us and asked us to go back indoors. He then made his way through the fine soft snow, knee deep in it, with his makeshift shovel in his hand. He climbed to the roof and began to shovel the piles of snow, throwing it into the side yard, while indoors we heard the thuds as it fell. He did not return to us until he had cleared the roof and prevented its collapse.

Another good thing about our house was that it was near the playground of Father Anthony's Monastery, and it took us only a few minutes to get there. All we had to do was to climb a wall at the back of our house, which my father, in order to make our climbing easier, had reshaped into steps. Then we took a path along the upper terraced plots, greatly shortening the distance to the playground. The entrance to the first of these plots actually led to the house of Butrus the Shoemaker, a strong, scowling, stiff-necked man. We were afraid to meet him accidentally because he would immediately ask us where we were going and whether we had trespassed on his property and stolen the last eggs that his hens had laid and whether we had let one of his rabbits escape. We never dared do anything of the sort because he had a big, ferocious black dog which he tied to a kennel most of the time. As soon as the dog smelled us at a distance, its frightful barking would bring its owner out.

Butrus the Shoemaker, who had a shoemaker's shop in the Anatira quarter, was bothered by cats. In spite of his big dog, they often raided his chicken coop and his rabbit warren. He had mastered the art of chasing cats with a club or an iron rod, and if a cat fell in his hands, he put it in a bag, firmly tying the opening. Then he caught a second cat and perhaps a third, forcing them into the bag with the first one. Finally he dashed the bag against a rock with amazing violence, while the cats screamed. We did not know whether he later buried them or burned them or carried them to the nearby garbage heap. Some said that he extracted their intestines and dried them, and used them for sewing his customers' shoes!

People thus considered him an expert in getting rid of cats and consulted him whenever they needed help in this regard. He might even volunteer his services, especially to his neighbors. That is what he did when he came to us one day, carrying his club and his ominous bag, and said, as his eyes roamed about our house, "I have seen a very agile he-cat at your house."

"No, this is our cat, Fulla," we said. "She lives with us inside the house and kills the rats."

"Nonsense," he said. "You don't see her when she climbs to our house and devours a chick or a little rabbit once in a while."

"Never, Uncle Butrus," we said. "She is well fed here, and she is content with living with us."

"I have come to rid you of her," he announced.

"God bless your good intentions," we answered. "But we don't want to get rid of her."

"By God, you people don't deserve to be served!" he shouted angrily as he nervously put his bag and club under his armpit and returned home.

Next to Butrus the Shoemaker's house was a small, two-roomed, old house built on the edge of a terraced plot over-looking the road. Uncle Hanna Dhiban and his family lived there. Exactly the opposite of his neighbor, he was a blind man who sat cross-legged on a rock near his door, receiving the greetings of passersby. He was a merry person, often telling funny stories or strumming his lute and singing.

Like us, his children played in the Monastery's playground. They were also members of the Boy Scouts and the band. Iskandar, the youngest, was a friend of mine in the Cub Troop. His father and two or three of his friends used to be invited to entertain at weddings. They formed a musical band: one of them, a carpenter, played the violin; another, an upholsterer, played the tambourine; the third, a tinsmith, had a beautiful voice and sang *mawwals* well. Iskandar took me to some of those weddings to enjoy the singing and the music of his father and his band. In front of them glasses of *arak* and small plates of *mazza* were set on a small table: that was all the fee they asked for.

In those days, there was no radio with singers singing day and night *ad nauseam*. All people sang, or at least they tried to, whenever they were moved. Weddings, however, were special occasions for hearing good singers accompanied by the lute, the violin, the hand drum, and the tambourine. Listeners joined in with particular enjoyment because a long time might pass when the only good singing heard would be in the mother-of-pearl workshops where the skilled pearl craftsmen, sitting on the ground, sang collectively to the rhythm of their saws, awls, files, and hammers but, of course, without the accompaniment of any musical instrument. Musical instruments were rare, and only at weddings did people have the good fortune of seeing and hearing instrumentalists. Whenever I passed by blind Uncle Hanna Dhiban on my way to the playground of the monastery, I imagined him playing his lute and singing, filling the street with cheer.

Teacher Jiryis returned from Syria at this time, my parents and all my friends' parents having waited very long for his return. It was good news to them for more than one reason: he was their children's teacher and his knowledge of Arabic, Syriac, and English was well certified; he was also the deacon of the church and known for his velvety voice which transformed the divine liturgy every Sunday morning into a small paradise of delightful chanting.

The only large room on top of the "ruin" was transformed into a school. Toward the end of the Ottoman period, the leaders of the Syriac Community had bought this old "ruin" near the municipal market. Perhaps it had once been a large palace, for it had many interconnecting, tiered rooms, but now it was in ruins, and the doors and windows of the ground-floor rooms were choked with heaps of fallen stones. When the stones were removed, musty odors of decay, the smells of bygone times, rose into the darkness that had not been touched by the sun for many years.

Before school started and during holidays, we played in this ruin called "the Church ruin," inasmuch as we dared to brave the putrid odors and the darkness. We imagined it was haunted and that a genie protected it and blocked the way of anyone who would enter. Challenging the genie and the demons was a courageous act not without danger. A challenger might return terrified after a short while, swearing that he had seen the white figure of a giant demon who was about to crush his skull with a large stone, had he not been able to slip out of his hands. More than once, I challenged the demon when my friends were not looking and probed into some of the ruined rooms, but fortunately for me or unfortunately for the demon, we never met. Yet being terrified was exciting and ended only with my coming out into the light to resume a game of "handspan" or "ear-of-corn" with the others. Meanwhile, several of our parents, who volunteered to work on the many days on which they were unemployed, would be busy carrying away the debris and the rubble on their backs and building the new church.

I might wrap my arm around the waist of the first friend I

saw, then we would both jump spontaneously, one of us shouting and the other responding, stressing the rhythm of the words.

"O Awniyya!"

"Where is the camel?"

"On the hilltop."

"What is he eating?"

"Sorrel seeds."

"What is he drinking?"

"Drops of dew."

And I always imagined that Awniyya was a dark Bedouin girl with black eyes and wine-red cheeks, whose braids flowed loosely over her breasts as she gave her beloved camel dew drops to drink from the palms of her hands.

Or I might challenge my friend with my spinning top if he also had one. This toy had a conical shape, tapering to a sharp point with a shiny nail in it. I would wind my thick thread around my top tightly, beginning at the pointed end and going upward to the broader part, which was decorated with colored circles, and my friend would do the same. Then we would yell, "One, two, three!" and spin our tops on the tile-covered floor with the greatest skill that we each had. The tops would spin on their nails with great speed, jumping and keeping their balance. The winner would be the one whose top went on spinning longer.

The "singing top," which was shaped like a capital T, needed greater skill because, after each had spun it off the leather string, he had to whip the string around its leg and then quickly withdraw it. This accelerated its spinning and dancing, and a soft humming would be heard as though the top were singing. The faster it spun, the more it danced and the louder it "sang."

The game called "strike-and-run" needed a large space of uneven ground. It was played with a long stick and a short piece of wood: the latter was placed on a hump on the ground so that one end of it was slightly higher than the other; one had to hit the higher end with a single stroke of the stick to make it leap into the air and, before it landed, strike it again forcefully so that it flew a long distance. One had then to run after it to where it landed and hit it again in the same manner. If a stroke failed to make it fly, the other person took over the stick to play his turn.

When the teacher rang the bell, our scattered playing ended, and we made for the only large and finished room, with its beautifully decorated floor tiles. The teacher sat at a table in front, on which reading and arithmetic books were neatly arranged, together with a number of sticks of various lengths and thicknesses with which to punish the lazy and the trouble-makers. Behind him was the blackboard, and on his right and left were two long windows. From the western window, which opened on the ruins, one could see the steeple of Father Anthony's Monastery and its clock, which rang the hours. From the eastern window, one could see the domes of the Church of the Nativity in the distance and the mountains beyond.

The boys sat at long school desks arranged in two blocks, between which was a central aisle leading to the teacher's table. There was enough space between the desks and the walls on the left and the right for students to squeeze in and go to their places. In each block, there were five or six desks, each of which seated five students, but seven, eight, or more could sit close together if need be. The older students occupied the front desks, and behind them students sat in descending order according to their classes.

The highest class, and the one nearest to the teacher, was the first class. My brother Yusuf was in it, as well as a number of older boys. Following behind was the second class, then the third, in which I was placed with about seven or eight of my friends. Behind us were two or three other classes for children between the ages of four and ten whom we called the "ABC children." Teacher Jiryis entrusted these to the "big" boys to teach them the Arabic alphabet and the first pages of the reader. There came a time when he also charged me with teaching a group of them to read. I was then eight years old, and that was my first experience teaching; it made me dream for many years after-ward of becoming a teacher as the best thing I could be in life.

The teacher dealt with us one class at a time: he called up

the members of one class to form a semicircle in front of his table, placing the cleverest nearest to him and arranging the others in descending order of marks so that the most stupid was at the end, and everybody called him "the tail." We would read to the teacher, and he would read to us. If he was angry at any boy because of laziness, he would make him step down two or three positions along the line of pupils or send him to the end of the line to be "the tail" and the laughing stock of everybody—that is, if he did not strike him once or more on the palm of his hand with one of the sticks on the table. If he was pleased with any one of us, he made us step up one or two positions or more, depending on the degree of his pleasure.

My brother kept his position at the head of the line of his class during the period he spent at that school. I sometimes occupied the first position and sometimes the second in the line of my class. However, from time to time the teacher would place in the first position the son of the prominent man who had given him a special room near the school, which he lived in with his wife free of charge. The fact that my brother remained at the top of his class was almost a miracle. Teacher Jiryis always said to Yusuf, "You remind me of my son Ibrahim! Your face, your gestures are the same as his! He went to America with his uncle and will never come back again." The truth is that my brother Yusuf rightfully deserved to be at the head of his class, although the teacher did not really go by the students' marks as he claimed, but by the importance of their parents and their social position in the community, despite the fact that they were all illiterate. His livelihood, let alone his monthly salary, depended entirely on their satisfaction.

A parent might pay a surprise visit to the school. The teacher would welcome him and make him sit in front on the chair he reserved near his own. He would make some of us come forward with our readers in front of the guest, including of course one of the guest's sons, who would be unexpectedly promoted to the head of the line, as though he were the first among us. The teacher would ask us to recite the lesson (this was his teaching method), and the guest would express his admiration for the classical Arabic language, of which he understood not a word. Naturally, the teacher would be invited to supper that evening or the next by the student's proud father, and it was customary that supper would consist in part of rice-stuffed chicken (in the days when chicken was the most expensive of meats), or else he would be displeased because he would consider the absence of stuffed chicken as an insult to his dignity.

It never occurred to my father to be a guest of the school. Likewise, he never tried to occupy a social position in the community that would make him prominent because he did not claim to be notable, nor did he want to be. When he did invite Teacher Jiryis to supper one day, the news spread quickly, especially among the women; and one of my mother's friends said to her, "If the teacher knows that you have not cooked chicken for him, he will go to supper with other people."

My mother was angry at such silly words (which the teacher later denied when my mother confronted him with her famous frankness) and said, "We will offer him whatever is available. He is free to come or not to come, to eat or not to eat!"

That disturbed me as it did my brother when we heard it because the teacher's visit to us was a means of promoting our position at school. A little while later, however, my mother asked us to catch and kill one of our chickens, the red hen which had stopped laying eggs, and to leave the rest to her.

The teacher came in the evening after my father had returned home from his work. In spite of our awe of the teacher, my brother and I were pleased to find he was talkative and merry, contrary to what we had expected. We all sat on the mat, while he sat on one cushion and leaned on another which my mother had taken down from storage. She put out salt-roasted watermelon seeds for him to nibble on, and he said to my father, "These two sons of yours have a very dear place in my heart. They will both become teachers of whom all Bethlehem will be proud. Yes, indeed."

My mother served him the rice-stuffed, roasted chicken with pleasure and joy. No member of the family touched it.

When after the coffee the teacher left, my mother said to my father, "How kind and gentle this man is! If he had asked me to give him two chickens, I would have surely done so! When he speaks, his voice is like magic to the heart; how much more so it will be when he chants. Next Sunday, I will go early to mass with you to hear him sing the hymns."

On the next day at school, the teacher was in a most cheerful mood. The classes went up to him, and he taught us our reading lessons in the three languages, one language at a time. One of the older students called Jalil, who looked like a grown-up man because of his height, was asked by the teacher to reread a sentence in the Arabic reader. He faltered and made many mistakes in reading it. The teacher was not angry but asked him to leave his position and step down to the beginning of the lowest desks where the "ABC children" sat so that he might study his lesson. The boy obeyed, and the teacher continued his teaching. But he noticed that Jalil was playing around with his new neighbors and making them laugh. Sitting behind his table, he rebuked him aloud and threatened to punish him by giving him four strokes with his stick if he continued to add bad behavior to his laziness. . . . Jalil gave in to the threat, but only temporarily, for soon he began again to make the boys laugh at his clownish gestures, which made the teacher shout, "Jalil! Come here and get your punishment!"

Jalil did not move from his place.

"Jalil! I told you, come and get your punishment!"

"I ain't coming," he shouted back defiantly, making all the school boys burst out laughing.

The teacher stood up and, with one of the thick sticks in his hand, walked in the direction of Jalil. When he was about to reach him, Jalil took a few steps backward. The teacher rushed to catch him, but the boy ran and protected himself in the narrow gap between the wall and the desks. The teacher became very angry and followed him. The boy ran from his spot toward the table, and the teacher followed him. Jalil then quickly entered the narrow passage between the other wall and the desks. As the teacher tried unsuccessfully to catch him, the other boys in class laughed uproariously. Jalil continued to run among the desks with the teacher following him, stick in hand, without being able to catch him, until the chase ended with Jalil bolting out of the door and disappearing.

Such rebellious behavior was rare because the students' parents sided most of the time with the teacher against their sons. A father would say to the teacher, pointing to his own son while we all heard, "This boy is not my son, Teacher Jiryis. He is *your* son. If he errs or misbehaves, beat him with your stick until he is set straight." In his melodious voice, the teacher would then repeat the adage over which fathers rejoiced, "The stick is for the disobedient."

And the disobedient among the boys were many indeed. Most of them came to school against their will and preferred to play among the ruins or roam about freely among the people in the nearby municipal market. However, the teacher knew his students: he knew who deserved to be treated well and taken care of and who deserved to be beaten and neglected. And there were those among us who were known not to fear any punishment, like Hanna "the lizards' friend," whose brother was in my class. Because of his laziness and bad behavior, this Hanna had to be struck several times on his palm daily. He received his punishment at the teacher's table, and as soon as the teacher turned his back to return to his place, he smiled vauntingly and made faces at the other boys, suggesting that he felt no pain; it was known that he used to catch lizards and rub his palms with their blood. We believed that lizards' blood strengthened the palm of one's hand and toughened its skin so that it did not feel pain when hit by the teacher's stick, regardless of how thick it was.

Not all the boys were as clever or as brave as Hanna in catching lizards, abundant as they were. Around noon time, when the sun flooded the walls of the terraced plots, we often saw a large lizard come out from among the stones to lie on a rock and face the warm sun; it moved its head up and down, and imagining it responded to our words with the movements of its head, we repeated:

Say your prayers, lizard,
Your father and mother
Are at the earthen oven.
Your father went uphill
To bring you some honey. . . .

I used to be happy to see the lizard steal away to its hole, having said its "prayers," before any of us harmed it.

We too said our prayers. The Syriac texts that Teacher Jiryis taught us were, for the most part, very old devotional lyrics and hymns which the early Church Fathers in Antioch, Damascus, Jerusalem, Edessa, and the cities of Mesopotamia had composed and set to music according to certain modes known to the clergy. The teacher taught us the seven variations on every basic melody, sometimes with the help of young monks from St. Mark's Monastery in Jerusalem or from Mosul. Every melody had seven variations, which were used on different days of the week and during periods of fasting and feasts. We had to learn by ear, without the benefit of notation—which ecclesiastical music developed in later years. The teacher made those of us with beautiful voices and musical ears the choir boys of the church.

There were two lecterns at the iconostas in front of the altar, one on the right and the other on the left, on each of which was a large manuscript. No one remembered when those manuscripts were written, they were so old. Those ancient Syriac books were a treasure which the church preserved with special care and great pride. Their leaves were very thick, and some were of parchment. Because of their weight and large size, the books could be lifted only with great effort. The texts were written in black ink, with the directions and rubrics in between the lines in red ink. If a book were to be lost, it would be impossible to replace it because of the scarcity of Syriac calligraphers.

The choir was divided into two semichoruses which huddled around one of the lecterns, and the chanted recitation alternated between them. Because of the intense darkness inside the church (it had not yet been supplied with electricity), one of the chanters always held a candle to light the text used by his half of the choir. Since the chanters stood in a circle around the lectern, the writing for some of them was completely upside down. Hence, we had to be able to read upside down, if necessary, and with the least amount of light available. Being probably the youngest member of the choir, I was often pushed around by the others to take my place in the circle where I had to read upside down!

Thus, I learned to read any text in Syriac or Arabic right side up or upside down equally well. But I took no special pride in that, for all my companions in the choir also learned to do so. It was very rare that any of us understood those texts, or even some of them. We actually prayed in a language which was mostly closed to us, in spite of the fact that we could read it right side up, sideways, or upside down, in the light or in no light at all.

6

"O Lamb of God, who taketh away the sins of the world, have mercy on us!"

The Lamb of God took away our sins and the sins of the whole world every Sunday morning, and often also on weekday evenings. But once a year, for one full week during Passion Week, He seemed to be exhausted by His pain and sorrow, and in a ritual manner associated with much chanting and music, the Lamb of God was sacrificed. He was tortured, humiliated, and lashed. He carried His heavy cross and went up to the top of Golgotha to be crucified with thieves. His blood flowed down the wood of the cross onto the skull of Adam, who had been condemned with his children to the eternal abyss. And the redeeming blood saved Adam, and us with him forever.

Passion Week was preceded by six weeks of fasting and prayer. We did our best to fast and pray for fifty days, every day of which we remembered His crucifixion and bitter sorrows at noon and in the evening. My father insisted during Great Lent that we all get up early in the day to kneel and pray two or three times before each of us left home, having had no food or drink. At school, which was next to the church roof, Teacher Jiryis concentrated on teaching us the hymns of Great Lent and the ones of Passion Week soon to come. They were all characterized by their sad and mournful modes. At midday, we all went down to the church to join Reverend Hanna or one of the other priests in prayers which differed from the prayers of the rest of the year not only because of their sad music but also because of the kneeling which accompanied them. The old priest, his long white beard trembling on his old black frock, knelt three or four times before succumbing to weariness. He turned round to us little boys and to a handful of men who had come to pray because they were unemployed. He reassured himself that, as we chanted to the rhythm of the kneeling, we actually knelt forty times in front of the drawn curtain of the altar, on which was painted Jesus crucified, with blood flowing from His palms, His side, and His feet onto a skull at the foot of the cross.

We used to boast that not one of us shirked his duties or cheated in performing them, though some did out of exhaustion. We also boasted that we knelt as many as forty times, our singing voices never failing though our stomachs were empty and our throats were dry, despite the dampness of the church which the sun hardly ever entered. No sooner would the priest finish giving the final blessings than we rushed outside, gripped by a wonderful hunger which made us quickly disperse in the roads as we ran to our homes. In those days, I realized that hunger was pleasurable when you knew there was food waiting for you, and that it was terrifying when you knew there was no food waiting for you.

My mother knew this perfectly well. She, too, fasted for half a day, and sometimes for a whole day until sunset. So did my grandmother, my father, and my brother. Mother was skillful in preparing simple hot lunches for us, consisting most frequently of lentils. She also cooked various kinds of vegetables in olive oil. Meat, fish, eggs, milk, cheese, and ghee were all

41

forbidden. We looked forward to Easter, the crowning event of Great Lent when all those foods were permitted again, if we had the money to buy them.

One thing I knew would be plentiful on Easter Sunday: eggs. I was responsible for collecting the eggs, which our active chickens laid in the spring. In my own way, I calculated how many eggs would be gathered in the special, large basket: Would there be one hundred and twenty or one hundred and fifty eggs? And I wondered, How many colors would we give them when my mother boiled them on Holy Saturday preceding the Feast of the Resurrection?

The Feast of Christ's Resurrection always came in the springtime. The neglected, terraced plots turned green, dotted with flowers of all kinds, which we simply called *hannoun,* anemones. There were yellow anemones, blue anemones, violet anemones. And there were those anemones of deep red that have the color of blood: poppies, which lifted their heads to the sun, their petals shining with dew. They shot up through rocks, thorns, and horrid weeds. They even raised their heads proudly from under the stone walls over which the cacti spread their thorny arrogance together with their delicate yellow blossoms, which transformed into fruits armored with thorns. In the shade of mulberry trees, apple trees, apricot trees, almond trees, and pomegranate trees, the poppies burst out of the brown soil like laughing wounds.

And under the olive trees of Wadi al-Jamal as far as one could see, among the yellow, blue, and violet anemones, poppies dotted the vast scene with drops of blood. In the wheat and barley fields, all along the road to Bayt Sahoor and on the land around it, poppies swayed with the green ears of corn, welcoming the thousands of birds swooping down on them from the blue sky, before rising again and vanishing in vast spaces bordered only by the far-away Blue Mountains.

In the evenings, flocks of swallows crossed the azure space, returning to the land they loved. Spring evenings in Bethlehem when we played or sang or told stories were noisy with legions of swallows, playfully flying in circles, swooping down on the roofs of houses, then rising to the open skies. We followed them with our eyes as they changed directions, and turned, and circled, and changed the direction of their flight again and again for reasons unknown to us. Not one ever collided with another as they wheeled and filled the skies with jubilation. Their joy entered our souls, and so we too exhibited intense movement and noise: we ran and jumped; we sang and shouted. Sometimes I lay down on the grass-covered ground to watch the thousands of swallows as they tossed among the clouds like waves. I tried to count them, and failing, I tried again and again.

The clouds were white like flocks of sheep, and I followed their magical transformations. As they stretched and expanded, the sheep turned into huge whales, then into strange eagles, the forefeathers of their wings spreading out motionless across the blue distances. I sometimes continued to observe those thin clouds till their edges turned red with the light of the sunset and then were transformed into marvelous pools of molten gold. When the full moon rose and ascended in two or three hours to its zenith, the white clouds stood in array around it in amazing concentric circles, as though they were sheep again or, now that they glistened, as though they were the fine fragments of pearl oyster shells, from which we carved crosses and pictures and statues.

Our pleasures were not all visual. We killed birds with slingshots, notably goldfinches and sparrows. And what boy was ever without a slingshot? Or what boy ever failed to make two things skillfully: a slingshot and a paper kite? The seasons for both were spring and summer. With the paper kites, whose tails we fashioned into different shapes, colors, and lengths, our imaginations rose to heights that birds could not possibly reach. From the roof of our house, I held the string of the kite, if I actually succeeded in making it fly and its tail did not fail me. I helped it to soar and remain in the air swaying like a bride, with its bangles fluttering like jewelry on a bride's breast, which I could hear even from that great height. And I continued to give more string to this kite that seemed to bear my dreams and fantasies higher and higher.

I do not deny that in making kites and flying them I was more skillful than in killing birds with a slingshot. I felt no joy when I hit a bird and it fell to the ground and I rushed to it and saw it struggling in its blood. Whenever I hit a bird, I ran to it hoping to find that it had fallen without being harmed. But that was a rare event.

In the early mornings, we hurried to a place near Prophet David's Wells where we dug in the damp earth and found worms that we put in empty match boxes. We used them as bait in small metal traps that we set up under the trees. If we were fortunate, a bird fell upon the trap in two or three days. Because we often opened the match boxes and found that the poor worms had died, we tried filling the match boxes with damp soil and putting in only one worm, and it remained alive till we forgot about it or lost it. But I inevitably returned to the flying swallows and the clouds that looked like sheep lost in the fields of the sky. And I refused to kill any birds.

And remnants of melodies from Great Lent and Passion Week echoed within me: O Lamb of God, who taketh away the sins of the world, have mercy on us! Have mercy on people, on flowers, on birds! Save us from death and the eternal abyss, so that we may all continue to contemplate the universe You have created for us, the universe that has such wonders, such diversity, and such infinite beauty, without end.

There are many monasteries in Bethlehem, which is to be expected in the place where Jesus Christ was born. These monasteries belong to different denominations and reflect some of the variety that religious institutions in Europe have had since Emperor Constantine made Christianity the official religion of the state and the people in the fourth century A.D. The history of these monasteries also reflects the long conflicts which Christian sects have had among themselves over the centuries—

conflicts in which national factors played no less a role than doctrinal factors. This is in addition to the ancient conflict between East and West, and especially between the Arabs and Europeans, which continued for a long time. The victory of the Arabs over the Byzantines and the expulsion of the Byzantines from Palestine, Syria, Lebanon, Egypt, and North Africa occurred in this period, to be followed three centuries later by the Crusades, after the European forces withdrew from Palestine and Syria for about seven hundred years, only to return once more in another form—the British and the French mandates at the end of the First World War in 1918.

However, the European religious connection to the Holy Land was maintained, in one way or another, in a variety of arrangements made during the four centuries that the Ottomans ruled Palestine. The Great Powers were always party to such arrangements, from czarist Russia (which considered itself the successor of Byzantium in the continuation of the Holy Roman Empire) to Britain, France, Italy, and Germany (each of which had its own religious institutions); the Ottoman Sultanate approved these arrangements in order to avoid armed conflict. Nevertheless, conflicts did flare up outside Palestine from time to time, the most severe being the Crimean War with its many political complications of which the religious question was only one element. This war broke out in the middle of the nineteenth century, with Russia on one side and the Ottomans, the British, and the French on the other. When the British came to Palestine under the mandate, they adhered to the principle of the *status quo ante*—but only with regard to religious institutions, as both ill fortune and ill intention would have it.

At the beginning of the 1920s, the important monasteries which gave Bethlehem much of its cultural and social character were Greek Orthodox, mainly represented by the original part of the Church of the Nativity built in 326 A.D. by Emperor Constantine over the grotto in which Jesus Christ was born. Equally important were the Franciscan monasteries, the most important of which was the Star of the East Monastery, which the local people called the "Eastern Convent"; it consisted of the Church of St. Catherine, which was attached to the Church of the Nativity. In it was the cave in which St. Jerome lived when he devoted himself to the translation of the Holy Bible into Latin toward the end of the fourth century A.D. Furthermore, there were the Salesian monasteries, the largest of which was a convent built in the nineteenth century on a hill at a short distance from the Church of the Nativity. It was called the Don Bosco Convent, but the local people called it Father Anthony's Monastery, Deir Abuna Anton.

The Franciscans represented the monastic order established by St. Francis of Assisi, which was mostly French in character and language, although originally founded by an Italian. The Salesians, on the other hand, represented an Italian order founded by Antonio de Sales in the middle of the nineteenth century. There were, of course, other Christian groups with small or large churches, such as the Greek Catholics, the Syrian Orthodox, the Syrian Catholics, the Armenians, the Lutheran Protestants, and others. Each of these monasteries and churches had its own school, and despite the primitive nature of many of them, they at least taught the elements of reading and writing among the younger generation growing up at the beginning of the 1920s.

One of the most beautiful things achieved by some of the convents of Catholic nuns was the establishment of elementary schools for girls, which, no doubt, were among the first schools for girls in the Arab world. The students in these schools wore elegant black and white uniforms, perhaps suggested by the habits of the nuns. The streets of Bethlehem acquired a special splendor when these school girls spread out at lunch hour or at the end of the school day in the afternoon, or whenever they walked in orderly lines going to church on Sundays and feast days. Although French was emphasized in these schools, the time soon came when the emphasis would change to Arabic.

The Greek Orthodox institutions still showed the Greek influence by the use of Greek in prayers. On the other hand, Catholic institutions, whether French or Italian, used Latin as their language of worship, and so the Arab Roman Catholics among Bethlehem's population were called the Latins. Other religious groups used their own languages in their prayers, too. But national consciousness, expressing itself increasingly since the middle of the previous century, made Christian Arabs insist on introducing more Arabic into all these prayers. The 1920s and 1930s witnessed the Arabization of most of the Christian worship services all over Palestine, although Latin and Greek remained the ritual languages used, next to Arabic, in many of the major old monasteries. Likewise, Syriac continued to be used with Arabic, as it had been for over one thousand years. The convent which preserved the continuity of this language was in the Old City of Jerusalem, namely, St. Mark's Convent, which was established in the fifth or sixth century A.D., and it boasted of being built on the ruins of the older church established by St. Mark on the site where Christ had the mystic Last Supper on the eve of his crucifixion.

The Muslims living in Bethlehem itself at that time were much fewer in number than the Christians. Most of them had belonged originally to certain neighboring villages, and some to a quasi-Bedouin tribe that had begun to be settled gradually in campsites to the east of Bethlehem. They were known as Bani Taamar. Their livelihoods and their relations with the people of Bethlehem led them to trade their tents for stone houses, and many of them later lived in the town itself. The mosque of Bethlehem, opening on the Square of the Monastery's Gate, was an important landmark in the town, going back to Ottoman times and, perhaps, to a much older period.

The severe poverty which befell Palestine toward the end of the nineteenth century caused the young men of Bethlehem to immigrate in large numbers to South and Central America. The First World War further increased the people's poverty and misery. At the beginning of the 1920s, the effect of immigration was clearly visible in the many vacant houses and buildings whose owners had left and in the state of disrepair and neglect, which characterized hundreds of homes and surrounding fields of the town.

However, the position of Bethlehem as the birthplace of

Jesus Christ gave it a unique distinction and offered a large number of its people the opportunity to earn an income from selling handicrafts associated with the Christian and Muslim holy places to tourists. The town imported large quantities of raw mother-of-pearl shells, which were transformed by the dozens of little workshops scattered along the main roads into rosaries, crosses, miniature models of the Church of the Nativity and the Dome of the Rock, in addition to boxes and picture frames studded with mother-of-pearl. Foreign visitors eagerly bought these goods. But there wasn't a single hotel in town, perhaps because of its proximity to Jerusalem. When foreigners were obliged to spend two or three nights in town, they stayed at a hospice attached to this or that monastery, and this continued to be the case until the end of the 1950s.

Another distinctive feature of Bethlehem was its Saturday market. Being a very old center of trade for a large district south of Jerusalem, the town was the meeting place of thousands of villagers and Bedouins every Saturday, beginning in the early hours of dawn. They gathered in its famous marketplace called, for some unknown reason, the Drain Market, later officially named the Municipal Market after it was reconstructed and reorganized. Saturday was more like a festival day, and the streets of the town were crowded with people who had come to buy and sell. In the marketplace itself, men and women mixed with sheep, goats, horses, donkeys, and camels in such close proximity that movement was almost impossible. Baskets of eggs and chickens jostled baskets of vegetables; and bags of wheat, barley, millet, and hay pressed up against cans of molasses, dates, pressed-sesame dregs, olive oil, ghee, and sesame oil. Many buyers and sellers were women in their flowing blue, green, and red dresses embroidered with bright colors, and their shouts and laughter filled the air and added a special radiance to this weekly festival. In my childhood, one of the most famous personalities dominating the market was a woman of strong character from the Karra'a family: she was corpulent, and her voice thundered as she acted like a charitable despot. Whenever difficulties and disputes arose, they were referred to her. She had a sharp tongue, and woe betide those who were not content with her judgments!

On this one day of the week, the shops of the town made as much money as on the other days of the week put together. It was the day for the grocer, the barber, the bleacher, the tinsmith, the seller of *halawa* (a sesame-cream sweetmeat bought by visiting villagers in large quantities), and the tanner. The last named was one of the prominent craftsmen of the town, his handiwork ranging from shoes (which were more like the old Arab slippers, but crudely made and very sturdy, and thus eagerly sought by tribesmen) to bandoleers, saddles, and halters for horses and donkeys.

Leather craftsmen traded also in daggers of different sizes and shapes. No Bedouin or quasi Bedouin was ever seen without a club hanging from his wrist, having a round boss studded with lead and nails; nor was he ever seen without a dagger in the middle of his belt, a weapon to defend himself with as much as to boast of. And yet, as soon as he raised his club or unsheathed his dagger, he was seized by the police and ended up at the police station on the Square of the Monastery's Gate. And that could be followed by court action, or by "reconciliation" and a costly appeasement, a process involving him and his relatives that might drag on for endless months.

8

Father Anthony's Monastery had a large orphanage for boys, where basic professions were taught in addition to religious lessons. If the boys did not become monks, they graduated as smiths, carpenters, printers, tailors, car repairmen, or shoemakers. Salesian institutions tended to emphasize professions that responded to society's practical needs.

The monks responsible for the affairs of the monastery at that time were fond of the arts, especially music and theater. They trained their students to love these arts, which were relatively little known in the Bethlehemite society of those days. Boys with sweet voices were selected for the church choir and taught the basics of music and solfège so they could sing Gregorian chants and four-part Latin hymns dating back to the Italian Renaissance and the Baroque Period.

They also formed a band consisting of brass and wind instruments, all imported from Italy. This band played its exciting music on public occasions, and its uniformed members marched in the streets of the town in proper formations, with musical note sheets clasped to their instruments, preceded by drummers beating their rhythm, while others merrily blew their cornets, clarinets, and tubas with shining brass wound around their necks. Some of the band members were in fact townspeople who did not live at the monastery.

The monastery had an "outsiders" playground, open to town boys regardless of their religious denominations. Father Domaggi supervised the playground with real love. From time to time, he added new swings or provided interesting games and activities to supplement the ones already established; and thus the boys continued to come to the playground in large numbers and with sustained enthusiasm. He knew all the boys by name, and he had a young assistant who was no less caring than he was.

The playground opened its black iron gate at four o'clock in the afternoon, that is, after the boys had ended their school day. Before the scheduled opening time, boys often crowded at the gate next to the house of Baddour. They knocked on the gate insistently, hoping one of the monks would open it. Some of the boys clambered up the high stone wall, which was part of the rampart surrounding the monastery, and then climbed down into the playground when it was not time for play. This prompted Father Domaggi to plant broken glass on the top edge of the wall in order to prevent illicit climbing, which of course never deterred some of the more daring boys. On the inside, the wall was completely covered with a thick, green climber, bejeweled with golden flowers we used to call clocks because each had a colored round face, in the middle of which were two filaments resembling the moving hands of a clock. We used to pick them and sip the delicious, fragrant honey-tasting drop in the heart of the corolla at the bottom of the filaments.

On Fridays and Sundays, the playground was open from morning till night. When the evening bell rang, the boys who were playing had to file into the church, which had a statue of the Virgin Mary above the altar. They attended a short mass in which they sang Arabic and Latin hymns, accompanied by a small organ played by Father Domaggi's assistant. Father Domaggi then ended prayers with a short sermon in broken Arabic with an Italian accent, which made the boys secretly laugh, but which by dint of repetition they began to understand. Most often, the sermon revolved around subjects related to the playground; it also stressed the Virgin Mary's love for us and her protection of us, and the importance of praying to her when one experienced fear or worry for she interceded with God for us, and God never rejected her intercessions. On certain Sundays, Father Domaggi invited an eloquent Arab monk called Father Odeh to the afternoon religious benediction service, and he gave us a sermon in beautiful Arabic that appealed to us and made us ask Father Domaggi to invite this monk again and again.

One evening I returned home after one of these sermons with a worry that had never occurred to me. According to the preacher, I carried two angels on my shoulders as everybody else does. On my right shoulder was the angel of good, and on my left, the angel of evil. Both were constantly whispering to me, the former warning me and the latter tempting me. The angel of good repeated, "How beautiful piety and good deeds are!" And the angel of evil reiterated, "How pleasurable sin and evil deeds are!" Having always dreamt of seeing angels, I found myself now carrying two of them, whether I liked it or not, and never seeing them: one wanted to lead me to Heaven and the other was driving me into Hell.

In a later sermon, the preacher reassured us that a boy was not responsible for his sins so long as he was under nine years old. In those days I was seven or eight, and I thought, "Let the two angels fight over me! My father and mother are the ones responsible to God if He ever called me to account for what I did or said!"

But what was sin? What deed or speech was it that God would make my parents accountable for on my behalf? I had to listen carefully to the angel of good, if I could actually hear him whispering in my right ear. And I had to stop the whispering of the angel of evil or report him to the angel of good when he whispered.

When I asked my father, "What is sin?" he first laughed at my question, then said, "What has sin to do with you?"

I said, "The monk says, 'Keep away from sin.' Is it what the angel of evil says?"

My father said, "Sin, my son, is stealing and lying. Don't steal and don't lie. If you don't, you are safe from sin. There is one more thing: Don't repeatedly use God's name in vain. Don't keep swearing by His blessed name. Also, don't vilify others. . . . Vilification is a sin in God's eyes."

My father's commandments were difficult to keep, but I never forgot them.

The monastery had a Scout Troop consisting of the boys of the "outsiders" playground. My brother Yusuf belonged to it, and so did my eldest brother, Murad, for a short time. As for me, I belonged to the Cub Troop. I was issued a green outfit with a green cap on which was a badge bearing a wolf's head. I was also given long woolen socks that went up to my knees and a pair of thick shoes that I wore during rehearsals and parades. All these were kept for me in a locker in a special room for scout uniforms. After my troop participated in several exercises, Father Domaggi selected me to lead the company. So I used to stand at its head and mark time in front of him as he trained us and pierced my ears with his sharp rhythmic whistle. Standing directly under his beard, I saw the hair in his nostrils move up and down above his mustache with his loud inhalation and exhalation.

My later activities in the company included my being

trained to play the drum. For a while, I was trained to play the clarinet, but my lungs were not strong enough because I was too young or, more likely, because I was too thin, so I gave it up. I used to lead my troop by beating the drum which hung on my shoulders (probably disputed by the two angels of good and evil). Some of the scout reviews took place on the stage of the monastery; I used to be the boy who formed the top part of the human pyramid, standing on the shoulders of two Boy Scouts who, in turn, stood on the shoulders of three young men standing in line on the stage before the spectators. I was always afraid of falling as I saluted the people with two fingers in the manner of Cubs, and I secretly prayed to God and the Virgin to let me hold out there for those few critical seconds until the curtain came down.

In addition to all this, Father Domaggi had a cinema. He had transformed the room above the church into a hall for social activities, the most important of which was the showing of movies usually scheduled for Sunday evening after the benediction service. Those who had not attended the prayer service were not permitted to see the movie. And so interest in church attendance and in playground participation generally was best on Sunday afternoon. When the bell for prayers was rung, the large black gate was closed so that no boy who had not done his duty toward his Lord could infiltrate into the cinema.

We sat pressed together on the floor of that room in order to watch the silent movies with fascination while the projector whirred away in the back of the hall. In that room I spent some of the most delightful hours of my life, watching Charlie Chaplin, Maccist, and other comedians whose names I did not know and watching, again and again, scenes from Zulu Africa, with Tom and Cob hunting lions, tigers, and elephants in the jungles. In my imagination, I shared in their exciting hunts, horse riding, and voyages to great cities in sailing ships. What a wonderful world that room opened up to us as we sat cross-legged on its frayed rugs!

Father Domaggi operated the projector and simultaneously gave a running commentary. From time to time, titles appeared that no one but him could read, so he "translated" them for us in order to help us follow the story. However, commentary was not necessary after the same film had been shown for the fifth or tenth time: we would have memorized the story in every detail, movement, and gesture. But we enjoyed seeing the events repeated exactly as we expected. One of Father Domaggi's most delightful surprises on weekday evenings was when he ended his sermon at the conclusion of prayers by saying, as his eyes gleamed with delicious expectation, "And now, children, we shall all go upstairs to the cinema. . . ."

Perhaps it was as an effect of these films that George, Sulayman, and I—as boys of seven—would climb the big mulberry tree in the green plot of George's house. Having driven bent nails into the branches, we turned them right and left and imagined that the tree was an airplane and we were pilots, and that when we turned the nails the airplane lifted us up into the sky toward the stars. The higher we rose, the louder our songs became. Then we landed our airplane, jumped off the tree, and began looking for lions and tigers among the fig trees and behind the terrace walls, hunting down at least one animal before going back to the "airplane."

All this was possible in imagination. Yet our imagination aspired to something larger and more challenging. I had seen the sea only in the films at the monastery. The idea of a vast body of surging water fascinated me, but Bethlehem had no river, not even a stream, other than the piped spring water or Ayn al-Qanat, as it was called. I used to hear about Solomon's Pools, but they were far away, and admission to them was forbidden. My friends and I had no alternative but to make a sea, if we wanted the sea.

Making a sea occupied us for a long time. We decided to dig a sea where ships could sail in one of the green plots. Each of us brought a pickax or an adz, and we began to dig. Digging was not easy, but after many days of exhausting efforts, secretly kept from our other friends lest they should spoil our project, we succeeded in digging a good-sized pit. We had now to fill it with "surging" water. Nature came to our help when rain fell with so much wonderful abundance that we were prevented from leaving home. It rained all night long, and I was almost unable to sleep, being so beset by the visions of the sea that we would fill with ships.

Next morning, before the rain had completely stopped, I hastened to the spot where the pit was. I found it overflowing with water, though very muddy. I shouted, "The sea!" I ran to George's house to tell him the miraculous good news. We spent that whole day making paper boats, which we took to our sea and launched on the murky waves.

The abundant rain of that winter was both a blessing and a bane, for it gave us a sea for several days, but it later swept it away, almost leveling it off with the land surrounding it. Our feet sank in the mud many times as we played on the shore of our sea, and when we returned home we were scolded for having dirty feet. I had to pour water on my feet until they were clean before daring to step into the house, where my mother had set up a brazier on which she put the cooking pot whose rising steam diffused warmth all around. Mother was busy sewing by hand, grandmother was spinning the wool we had shorn from our sheep, and so I told them of the voyages I would make on the high seas when I grew older and became a man among men.

■　■　■

Every boy who frequented the monastery's playground had a small notebook with his name on it. Father Domaggi's assistant, the church organist, kept them in his possession. He was a jolly, young Italian man called Giuseppe, whom we nicknamed Beppe. He kept the notebooks in a handy box where they were arranged alphabetically. When we entered the church, he distributed them to us by name; and when we left, we passed by him as he sat behind the organ next to the door and gave them back to him. He stamped each book with the word "Present." As days and weeks passed, the notebook was filled with this word repeatedly stamped in regular tables representing the weeks and months. He who had the most of them quarterly or annually was favored with a better gift than the other boys at Christmas or other festive occasions. Two days before Christmas, the boys were asked to come to the playground in the afternoon. We met in the church for a short service, and then we were ordered to go to the room upstairs. We raced one another as we climbed the stairs and were surprised by a wonderful sight. In the middle of a low platform was a big tree decorated with stars, shining balls, twinkling electric bulbs, and colored tape. Next to it was a crèche with baby Jesus lying in a manger, his mother sitting near him, and St. Joseph standing at his head, while two cows and a donkey contemplated the miraculous baby with a bright halo and the angels fluttered above everyone in a circle. Around the tree and the crèche were dozens of gifts arranged in tiers on a ground covered with blue, red, and yellow paper.

We sat on the floor, and Father Domaggi told us how happy he was with our presence at the monastery and our regular attendance at church. The Virgin Mary, he said, had come to know us all, prayed for each one of us, and gave us her blessings every day.

Then Father Odeh rose and said in eloquent Arabic that his colleague Domaggi sought his inspiration from the life of Christ the Lord to reward each boy among us for coming to the monastery so that we would continue to come. Was it not Jesus who said, "Let the children come unto me, for the Kingdom of God is made of such pure ones"? Jesus was exactly like us: He was poor, and He was destitute. He was born in a cave in which animals were fed in the winter. It was bitter cold on the day He was born, and snow fell. His poor, exhausted mother put Him in a manger so that He could have some warmth. When He grew up, He walked in the streets of Bethlehem and Nazareth and Jerusalem barefoot like us, with few clothes on, mostly in tatters, a victim of the winter cold and the summer heat. Nature was harsh, he said, and we could not bear its harshness as Christ the Lord did; nonetheless, we had to follow His example in spite of everything. Blessed were the poor, for they would inherit God's Paradise.

Beppe then went up on the platform to distribute the gifts. He called our names, one by one, from a list in his hand. Burning with excitement, we went up to him and received our gifts. Mine was a pair of boots.

I ran home with my present, pleased with these boots whose like I had never worn. As usual, my brother Yusuf was with me. He too had received a present, but it was quickly forgotten. That evening, my boots were a source of joy; their beauty and strength and awesomeness outshone every other piece of apparel at home! The joy of my father, mother, and grandmother was not less than mine. In fact, my father, who claimed experience in shoemaking and had a tool box with an anvil, sharp knives, a hammer, and nails for the repair of family shoes, began examining the boots. He turned them over in his hands, smelled the leather, inspected the soles and the sewing like an expert, and finally gave his judgment that they were well made, and added, "No doubt, they were made by the skilled orphans of the monastery."

I put the boots on the window sill, one neatly next to the other, unable to admire them enough and yearning for the morning to come, in order to wear them.

At night, a disturbing thought occurred to me while everyone was fast asleep: Who said the boots would be my size? They could be too big or too small. I left my warm bed cautiously lest I should awaken my father, beside whom I slept. I groped my way through the darkness to the window. I took one boot and thrust my foot in it; then I took the other boot and put it on. I walked a couple of steps and felt the bite of the thick, cold leather on my toes: it was a delicious bite. The boots were exactly my size. I was reassured. I returned the boots to the window sill and stole back to my bed and slept peacefully until morning.

When I woke up, I wanted to wear the boots, but my mother said, "Why don't you leave them for Christmas Day, so you can wear something new?"

I said, "But Christmas Day is still too far away."

She said, "Only two weeks or less."

Christmas for the Orthodox communities, according to their Eastern calendar, came thirteen days after the Christmas of the Western calendar.

Our Christmas was preceded by a twenty-five-day fast. My parents observed the fasts as keenly as the holy days. Fasting for us solved problems in a way that pleased both God and man, for we abstained from eating meat, fish, eggs, greasy foods, and all kinds of dairy products. All these cost money, which we did not have. And so, we pleased God by fasting and made a virtue of necessity. At any rate, so long as there were bread, olives, and vegetables—which were always cheap—we were content and happy, however skimpy the amounts were.

However, when Christmas came, we had to have some meat, milk, and cheese with which to break the fast after attending the midnight service at the Church of the Nativity. In other words, we had to have some money to spend. My mother had to plan every day's expenditure, which was not exactly my father's concern.

In those days, my father was a construction worker. He carried building stones on his back, taking them to the mason after the chiseler had finely dressed their surface with his chisel and carefully shaped their angles. He was paid five or six piasters per day, and he gave what he earned to my mother to spend as her wisdom and experience dictated. Yet, however wise and experienced she was in spending the money, she knew she had to feed us and, in addition, to sew our clothes by hand, patch them, and make do with the few fabrics available to her, which were often parts of older clothes. When winter came, matters were more complicated. Construction work was hard to find, and my father spent days going from one construction site to another looking for work, and he returned home exhausted and hungry. He never complained. He stood up in a corner of the room to pray before going to bed: he thanked God for His blessings and would not lie in bed before he was sure that my brother and I had also said our prayers prior to taking off our clothes in order to sleep. And so we recited "Our Father Who Art in Heaven" several times as a prayer of thanks for God's favors.

How could I know that my new boots would sharply emphasize the problems of our daily survival? My father was without work, and despite our fasting, Christmas was coming soon and the few piasters saved were hardly sufficient to buy the lentils that we ate on most days of our fast, let alone buying what was more expensive and tasty. That was why, as I was told on my return from school at noon that day, my mother and father had agreed to sell the boots! She knew some well-to-do neighbors who would enthusiastically buy them for a reasonable price. The sale would provide us with money to buy some Christmas necessities.

I was not too happy with this logic. But it was difficult for me to argue with both my father and mother. Neither were they happy with the logic of need.

My mother said, "We will be able to sell the boots, and we will make sure to provide you with another pair."

"How? How?" I said crying.

"I'll take you to the city," she answered, "and I'll buy you shoes to fit you from the Jewish Quarter. They say shoes there cost no more than two piasters a pair."

My mother sold the boots on the next day for fifteen or twenty piasters. A day or two later when the rain had stopped and the sky was clear, my mother took me with her to the Square of the Church of the Nativity, and we climbed into a horse-drawn carriage. She insisted on seating me in her lap like a baby in order to avoid paying my fare of one piaster or even half a piaster. That was my first trip to the wonderful city— Jerusalem. And for the first time I saw Jaffa Gate, crowded with people and animals, and we went down the lane into the Suwayqa market. I could hardly believe that there were so many shops and people in the world or that they would be so noisy!

We walked in the arched narrow alleyways. Every time we turned a corner, the scene changed, and so did the smells and the sounds. Finally we entered an alley in which the shops on both sides huddled close to one another, their doors wide open; it seemed to me that all of them were full of used shoes, stacked in pairs on shelves rising endlessly above one another. That was the beginning of the Jewish Quarter, pungent with the strange smell of rot and decay. Through the open doors, I could see the inside of the houses between shops: men dressed in black with odd furry hats on, and women with children and chickens underfoot. The smell of chicken droppings dominated everywhere.

We entered a shop whose owner sat at the door behind a shoe-sewing machine. He was wearing a leather apron. When we asked him to show us what shoes he had in my size, he spoke in a strange dialect I did not understand. But my mother understood him and told me he spoke the dialect of the Jews of the Maghrib. In those days, it was enough to say of someone he was a "Moghrabi" to conjure up images of him as a mysterious magician harboring evil designs. For the Moghrabi in our folk tales was usually the stranger who forced his way into the hero's life with the trickery of his cunning and witchcraft. That was why I was afraid of this Jew, as he brought down one pair of shoes after another for me to try on and my mother rejected them. Finally, she was pleased with a certain pair, and the shopkeeper said the price was exactly two piasters.

The shoes were patched, but the man reassured us that the patching had added to their strength and that I would be able to wear them for years.

"Come on! What nonsense!" my mother said in her worldly wise way. "Don't you see he is a child? His feet will grow, and your patched shoes will be good for nothing in six months."

We did not find any unpatched shoes at that price. So we gave up, and I surrendered my feet to the miserable pair of shoes. We returned to Jaffa Gate, climbed into a carriage, and waited for one hour before other passengers came. Meanwhile, I kicked the carriage floor with my shoes to accustom my feet to them.

No one at home liked my "new" shoes, so I shook them off my feet as one does fetters. And I ran barefoot toward the "sea," which had not yet been completely washed away. I felt the evil angel fidgeting and clearing his throat on my left shoulder, and I thought he was about to say something I ought not to hear. The good angel remained silent as I splashed the water with my freed feet.

On the day before the Orthodox Christmas in the Square of the Church of the Nativity, there were noisy celebrations welcoming the Greek Orthodox Patriarch on his arrival from Jerusalem in a great procession. He was received by a brass band, platoons of policemen and cavalry, files of Boy Scouts, choirs and long-haired priests, and carriers of holy banners. Hundreds of children in new clothes or in old rags shared the joy and noise of the feast day. On the sides of the Square, vendors of white halva, sesame bars, and *ghrayba* and *maᶜmool* cookies hawked their wares in honeyed shouts. My friends and I never got tired of watching and playing in this festival.

The night before Christmas, though fatigued by staying up late, we slept no more than three or four hours because of our eager anticipation of dawn. My mother awakened the family members, turning up the wick of the kerosene lamp and saying, "Don't you hear the angel's bell?" That was the bell in the belfry of the Church of the Nativity, which rang and filled the air with its sound announcing the last part of the night.

Without hesitation, my father, my brother Yusuf, and I got up from bed and put on our clothes. My mother made me wear two coats, one over the other, and we went out into the darkness. We hurried to the Church of the Nativity, blowing into our hands because of the severe cold.

In the intermittent drizzle, the Square glittered with its few electric lights and their reflections shining in the water that had gathered in the cracks between the large flagstones. The halva vendors were still on the sides of the square, sheltering themselves from the rain as best they could by the high stone walls. Those who sold grilled meat fanned the charcoal fires of their braziers, which shed red light on their faces, and they hawked their goods. Chestnut sellers blew on their embers to roast their precious chestnuts and keep themselves warm. There were older men who carried huge pitchers almost as tall as they, at the bottom of which fires burnt in built-in braziers; they shouted, "Hot salep . . . Hot salep." People were in constant motion all over the place as though no one of them had gone to bed that night.

We entered through the low and narrow rock door into the vast Nativity Church with its very high ceilings. It was dark inside in spite of hundreds of colored oil lamps in which small flames flickered like stars among the giant, smooth, marble columns. The towering altar was aflame with candles with thousands of worshipers and pilgrims crowded before it as the choir chanted the Byzantine liturgy in harmony with the continuous ringing of the mighty bells above the roof of the basilica.

We met many of our acquaintances who had come like us to attend the postmidnight service. Through the dense crowd of men, women and children, we made our way down the slippery, marble steps leading to the cave in which Christ was born. Warmed with the breath of worshipers, the air was redolent with incense and candle fumes. The venerable priest read the Christmas story from the Gospel in a scratchy voice affected by old age. It was as though he was reading it for the first time: he mentioned the shepherds who sought warmth with their sheep one night when snow covered their pastures in the fields and the hills, and lo, the angels suddenly appeared to them, lit up the sky with their radiant light, and gave them the good tidings that a savior was born unto them in Bethlehem and sang, "Glory to God in the highest, peace on earth, and goodwill among men!"

When we left the Church and the hymns were far behind us and the ringing of bells diminished, the rising sun was struggling with the clouds in the distant blue horizon. I looked at it with great pleasure, imagining the heavenly hosts filling the universe with their music and their good tidings, as though I had finally seen them with my own eyes.

At home again, I found that my mother and grandmother had begun cooking the Christmas meal. Steam rose from a big pot on the kerosene stove, the Primus. I smelled the delicious meat my mother had bought with the money remaining from the price of my beautiful boots, which I had forgotten in the noise and hubbub of the feast and its music.

Everyone was happy with the food they ate that morning after a hard fast that lasted twenty-five days. When we finished eating, my mother began pulling the "tablecloth" from the floor, and my father said as he withdrew to his reclining position on the pillow, "I wish you hadn't sold the boots, Maryam. We've deprived the boy of them, and it's a feast day."

"What was done was done," my mother replied. "Besides, by God's grace, you're here, Abu Yusuf, and you'll buy him a thousand boots in the days to come."

For many years afterward, whenever Christmas came, I remembered those boots which I never wore. But I soon forgot them in the overwhelming joys of the feast—or in the overwhelming sorrows which it cruelly brought with it in some years, without mercy.

9

For children and for adults, Naoom was one of the characters of the neighborhood. The children liked him: he was their friend who played and exchanged pranks with them. The adults always found him "between their feet" in the streets, in the houses, with the young women, and with the old hags.

He had a large body but his face was a child's, despite his fourteen years of age. His left arm was almost paralyzed, the forearm always raised to his waist. His left hand appeared as though it was merely suspended from his wrist, its fingers twisted and shriveled into the palm, and it was smaller than his unimpaired right hand. Day in and day out, he wore a long striped *qunbaz* which reached his ankles and acquired a new patch now and then. When he walked, he dragged his left foot, which was not as able as his unimpaired right foot. And so he was obliged to stagger as he walked, yet he advanced forward with amazing speed. In fact, one of his favorite games was to challenge us to race him, and he won most of the time.

I was seven or eight years old when I became aware of him or when he began to mix with me and my friends. He often came to school and asked Teacher Jiryis to teach him how to read, which made the boys laugh and cheer noisily. The teacher made him sit in one of the desks but soon forgot him. When he got bored, he stood up, which made the boys laugh again, and he left to wander in the streets. Since school was next to the market, he went there and found one woman or another who gave him her basket to carry home for her, with the vegetables she had bought; in return, she would give him half a piaster or some food.

The Dabdoub Close on the edge of the neighborhood had many rooms, each with a family in which the old and the young, the women and children, the chickens and rabbits all mixed. If he happened to go to any one of those families and was given food, he loitered as he moved from family to family, carrying a baby girl here and picking a quarrel with a child there. The women shied away from him and chided him saying, "Come on, Naoom. Get going, boy. Move on, we have work to do." They were embarrassed by his presence, for they squatted on low stools to wash clothes or to prepare food, and their legs and thighs showed. But he would not go away easily, or if he left, it was only to enter another house. Children gathered around him, their mothers prodding them to make fun of him, so they would say, "Dance, Naoom, dance!" So he danced as they sang, "The big bear got up and danced / And killed no less than seven souls. / The big bear got up and danced."

He came running to my house once, took me by the hand, and said panting, "Would you like to see a bear? Come with me, quick, before he goes away."

I ran with him to Abu Shamoon's café, where we saw a circle of boys, men and women blocking the road, forming a circle around a gypsy who was making a bear dance. In one hand the gypsy had a tambourine, and in the other he had a stick and the end of a rope connected to a ring which pierced the bear's nose. They moved about in the middle of the crowd: the gypsy commanded the bear to stand up, so he stood up on his hind legs. He gave him the stick, and the bear held both ends, resting it on his shoulders behind his thick neck. The gypsy rapped on his tambourine, and the bear swayed and danced as the spectators laughed and made funny remarks.

I had a strange feeling that the bear actually looked like Naoom! I looked at my friend and saw how fascinated he was by the animal swaying in front of him as the gypsy shook the rope now and then. The bear shook his head and continued his clumsy dance to the rhythm of the tambourine, then suddenly returned to all fours and lurched around the circle of spectators. Meanwhile, his owner turned his tambourine upside down and went around among the laughing spectators in order to receive a few coins as the crowd began to disperse.

Naoom never missed an entertaining act. Being one of the permanent fixtures of the neighborhood, he learned all he needed to know about it in his own naive way. There wasn't a boy or a girl or a man or a woman whose name, residence and, relatives he did not know. From the moment we moved into our home in the Dabdoub Close, with its large gate almost directly opening on Ras Iftays Street, Naoom never wanted me to miss an opportunity to see a dancing bear or a monkey act. Monkeys and baboons came to Bethlehem more often than bears, and they had better tricks to make people laugh—and give away their measly piasters. The monkey man was an artist of a special kind, and between him and the monkey (or monkeys), there was real understanding. Naoom said to the monkey man, "Tell the monkey to show how a woman sleeps."

The man silenced him with a dramatic gesture of his hands, then addressed the monkey saying, "And now, brave monkey, show this respectable crowd how an old woman sleeps."

The monkey lay down on his side, with his head bent down on his chest and his knees pulled up to his belly, and he snored in his "sleep." The crowd laughed, while the monkey man dramatically moved in their midst, waving his cane. He then addressed the monkey again saying, "And now, brave monkey, show this respectable crowd how a young woman sleeps."

The monkey lay on his back and moved his head slowly right and left, his straightened legs thrown wide apart. Everyone laughed again, Naoom the loudest of all. And I did not exactly understand why they were laughing.

No season of the year passed without a visit to the town by

troupes that attracted circles of people around them. The entertainments might last an hour or two, especially if the troupe was one of magicians. A magician would say, "My hand in the air is empty." Suddenly, he would be holding eggs, colored balls, or rabbits. He would stuff a handkerchief in his mouth, releasing the end of a thread from between his lips moments later. His helpmate took hold of it and pulled, and, lo and behold, he pulled out a succession of handkerchiefs, little flags, iron trinkets, and rusty razor blades from the magician's mouth. The thread lengthened and lengthened, endlessly coming out of the magician's interior with the objects hanging from it. After this, the magician swallowed swords and spit out flames of fire. It was in those days that I heard the adults speaking about Saleem al-Ashee (a friend of my eldest brother, Murad, at the time), who had a small shop on Manger Square for renting and repairing bicycles. They began to call him Saleem the Magician because of the wonderful tricks he performed in evening parties to entertain the elders of the town. When I first saw him, he was a short young man with an unsmiling lean face and amazing big eyes that shone brilliantly.*

I was fascinated seeing a group of gypsies consisting of three women who danced and two men who played musical instruments. The women danced and sang in front of Abu Shamoon's café. Although I had often seen people dance and play music in weddings, the gypsies were different, for the women, in their colorful and flowing dresses, moved freely, tenderly, and with a coquetry I had never seen; and the player of the long-necked lute filled the street with his resonant music diffusing merriment and joy. Of course, Naoom was the first to arrive at such a "party" and the last to leave it. When spectators showered half-piaster and mil coins on the gypsy dancers, Naoom picked some up from the ground nimbly, despite his

---

*This self-taught young man soon became a legend because of the amazing feats of hypnotism he performed and his ability to communicate with the spirits through his sister, who was a medium. This happened after he had gone to Jerusalem and then to Beirut, where he called himself Dahish Bey and then Dr. Dahish and founded a religious group known as the Dahishiyya.

limping movement, and dropped them at the dancers' feet as though he himself were generously giving them. Meanwhile, the dancers bent backward as far as they could, shaking their shoulders and their large breasts and letting their luxuriant hair flow to the ground, and they ceaselessly clicked their castanets as they sang. Wearing his Ottoman fur cap and baggy trousers, Abu Shamoon went among the crowd serving coffee, lemonade, and fizz to those who requested them.

The big event that was the talk of Bethlehem one season was the coming of the circus to town. It occupied the large square at the Municipal Market. My brother Yusuf took me to the place, and with us we took Naoom, Abdu, George, Sulayman, and others. At the market, we saw scaffolding being set up and ropes being tied from one mast to another, all amid hustle and bustle. Two or three days later, we attended a show that amazed me: in it I saw a man and a woman walk on a tight rope, high in the air across the market square. They also performed acrobatic acts on the rope, making me afraid they would fall—I felt as though I were the one about to fall into the bottomless pit!— but they did not fall. My brother said, "Look! The man walking on the rope has tied a bar of Nablus soap under each foot, and yet he does not slip or fall!" The young woman followed him on the rope with light steps, and I could see a golden tooth shine between her lips as she laughed. The sighs of the admiring onlookers could be heard as far as Manger Square!

Naoom swore that, if he were allowed, he would walk on the tight rope as the best acrobat would. We said to him, "We believe you, indeed, Naoom. But let us see you do it now."

Three or four days later, he came to take me with him in order to see the long-bearded snake charmer, around whom a circle of spectators had begun to gather. The charmer had put down the snake pouch he carried and started to play his flute when a large snake put its head out of the pouch, stretched its neck, and began to sway with the tune. Moments later, the heads of other snakes appeared next to it. Afraid yet delighted, Naoom held on to my arm, my fear and pleasure being not less than his own.

These exciting events that shook the street for one or two hours were few and far apart in time. Naoom was aware of that, and yet, despite his yearning for unexpected shows crowding the street, he was happy with the calm and warmth of the neighborhood and feared only the cold and rainy days. His favorite places were the thresholds at the entrances of large homes on the road. Made of big stones smoothed by time, these thresholds were often as high as stone benches, and their doors were seldom opened. Naoom sat on the edge of the threshold next to the corner, rubbing one bare foot with the other and watching the passersby as he waited for his friends to come out of school. He always had a few candies with him, a handful of salted and roasted watermelon seeds or chickpeas, or a number of cigarette butts which he gathered from the streets, kept in an old box, and offered to this or that old lady who sometimes took care of him. He possessed tin boxes of various kinds and sizes, which he obtained from the garbage dumps. There was such a dump near the Frères' School, and he went to it from time to time like one looking for a treasure and came back with all sorts of refuse, boxes, and bottles which he generously offered to his friends in return for their playing with him.

On a hot day, I saw him shortly after noon sitting in a shady corner of a large gateway. He staggered as he rushed toward me saying, "My patience ran out waiting for you. Don't you ever leave home?"

"I was at school this morning," I said. "This afternoon, there are no classes."

"Where are you going?" he asked.

"To George's house, so that we may go to the terraced green plots together," I replied.

He asked, "And where are the sheep?"

"My father sold them last week," I said. "He is now looking for two new lambs."

He took my hand and said, "I'll come with you to George's house, and we'll take him with us to the garbage dumps."

I said, "It is hot and my eyes are hurting."

He said, "I have found a new garbage dump other than that of the Frères. And let me tell you, it is astounding! It is near the dome, and it is chock-full of things. Come on!"

We ran to George's house and found him sitting on the ground in front of his father, with a book in his hands. His father was urging him to read it, his big pipe hanging under his thick mustache, emitting circles of smoke, and a headkerchief, without a black rope, wrapped about his head and neck. As soon as George saw us through the open door of the house's courtyard, he put down his book and came out to be with us.

We headed for the trench on the edge of the courtyard, descended into it, leapt from there to the main road, and started walking toward the dome. The dome is one of the principal landmarks of Bethlehem, and to me, it was the dividing point between the known and the unknown. So long as I remained on this side of it, I was within the bounds of the town that I knew and that knew me. But if I went beyond it, where the road stretched all the way to Jerusalem, I was venturing into a world full of secrets and mysteries. Near that place, there was a stone on which was written "Municipal Limits of Bethlehem," and it confirmed my sense of the dividing line between the familiar and the strange.

The dome was a small, cubical building topped by an actual dome. In its low wall bordering the road, there were two small windows that were always open because they had no shutters. The full name of this building was Rachel's Dome. My brother had told me that Rachel was the mother of Handsome Joseph and that, when she was traveling with her husband, Jacob, she died on the road and was buried there, leaving a baby, called Benjamin, who was two days old.

Sometimes we saw strange looking men wearing long, black overcoats and black fur caps or hats. Their faces were sullen, and they had long beards and slight, spiral ringlets for sideburns. We called them *hakhams* (rabbis). They came to the dome in cars, and we heard their strange wailing as they prayed inside. We hardly approached the two windows to look in before we backed off with some mysterious fear. Our mothers continually warned us against those Jews, saying they kidnapped children in Jewish festivals in order to slay them and mix their blood in the dough of unleavened bread. We saw them many times and were surprised that no one ever dared to lay a hand on us. Of course, we did not give them the opportunity to do so by coming closer to them than was necessary.

It was very hot that day. My eyes had been sore for the last two or three days, and my eyelids itched and hurt. I felt that the way to the dome was very long this time, and the bright, white soil unusually dazzling. I was sweating all over and felt my sweat trickle down my temples, my neck, my back, and my buttocks. Meanwhile, Naoom continued to tell us about the treasures of the garbage dump he recently discovered until we reached an old hut shortly before arriving at the dome. Its front was festooned with a green vine from which bunches of unripe grapes were hanging. Suddenly, Naoom yelled, "The she-bear! The she-bear is coming out! Take care!"

A corpulent and ugly woman came out to sit under the vine trellis. It seems she was concerned about her grapes, for whenever anybody came close to them, she assailed him. We had to pass in front of her vine trellis in order to turn off the main road to Naoom's treasures. Naoom shouted at her, "How are you, bear?" and threw a pebble at her and dashed off despite his limp. We began running behind him. The woman came out, throwing stones at us and yelling at us in a husky voice, "You thieves! You sons-of-bitches!" And I imagined her thick lips following us and hurling that continuous, mad bark at us from under her frightful mustache.

Panting, we reached the garbage dump. The heat and sweat were causing my buttocks to become even more inflamed, and my tears flowed because of the terrible, itching pain in my eyes. I had to avoid the pieces of broken glass and knife-sharp metal fragments as I moved in my bare feet and rummaged through the garbage with the others, looking for something to take back home. The stink was loathsome, and the flies skirred in clouds and settled on us and on everything. A short distance from us, the olive trees seemed clean despite the dust on them as they stood sleepily under the burning sun. My two friends leapt from pile to pile, now and then shouting, "Hey, look! See what I found!"

Having found nothing that I liked, I was sick of it all and walked away from the metal fragments, the shreds of cloth, and the bones to one of the olive trees on the other side, and I lay down on the red soil in the shade. How cool it was in the shade! I wished I could sleep on the ground. But Naoom and George kept shouting, and my burning eyelids and buttocks prevented me from relaxing.

We returned to our neighborhood as the sun was about to set. It was a trip of torture for me. On reaching his home, George left with several rubber heels and a broken mirror. Naoom left me at the large gate, on the threshold of which he sometimes spent the night, and his breast pocket was stuffed with all kinds of refuse. When I reached home, I was hardly able to walk.

My mother said, "With such inflamed eyes, where have you been, sweetheart? What is this strange redness in your eyes? Come, let me wash them for you." Turning to my grandmother, she said, "Mother, get me the eye drops." She then washed my eyes, sat on the floor, made me lie in front of her with my head in her lap, and put the drops in my eyes.

I then told her about the burning pain in my behind. She took off my pants and my underpants. After one look at the painful spot, she exclaimed, "What is this redness? Where have you been since noon in this condition?"

She brought a brass bowl of cold water and splashed my thighs and buttocks several times. She then emptied another bowl in the same manner, threw a piece of linen to me, and said, "Come on, dry yourself now . . . look at you, going around in the streets like a red-bottomed monkey . . . look at your legs and feet! It is as though you play nowhere but in garbage dumps! Get up and wash your feet like a decent human being."

I have never experienced pain as I did that night. All the members of the family went to sleep, but I continued to turn in bed next to my father. He became aware of my sleeplessness and asked me in the dark, whispering, "What is the matter with you? Why don't you sleep?"

I said, "My eyes are hurting a lot, Dad. My eyes, my eyes...," and I started weeping.

My mother woke up and said, "Hush, sweetheart, hush! I will put more drops in your eyes, and you will feel better. Just one moment."

She got up and raised the lowered wick of the lighted kerosene lamp, and I felt as though the light was about to blind me. She took me again into her lap and put more drops in my eyes. She then rose and lowered the wick. In those days she was still nursing my brother Issa, and so, when she noticed that I did not sleep, she placed me beside her, took out her breast, and squeezed drops of her milk into my eyes. As a result, I felt somewhat cooled and comforted.

But hardly had I gone to sleep in her arms when I woke up again with the burning pain in my buttocks and my eyes, and an involuntary groan in my throat. My parents and grandmother discussed what to do: my father suggested that we wait till the morning; my mother said that I was very sick; and my grandmother commented that there should be some medicine better than those silly eye drops.

When they had come to a consensus, my father said to me, "Can you pee?"

I said, "I will try."

My mother gave me a brass bowl and said, "Pee in it!"

She then brought the dropper, filled it with my urine, and generously dripped the urine into my eyes.

She wiped my eyes and cheeks and laid me beside her again while my baby brother was in the cradle on her other side. She patted me on the chest and sang a lullaby to me as if I were another suckling babe. And I slept.

When I woke up in the morning, I found I was alone on the mattress spread out on the floor. The door was open, and through it, I saw the courtyard of the close glistening and the distant blue mountains behind it shining. I ran my hand over my eyes cautiously. The pain had gone as though by a miracle. I heard noise coming from the neighbors; the women were laughing and clapping and singing, "The bear got up to dance and, doing so, he killed seven persons. . . ." I got up quickly, put on my pants, and went out to join them in clapping for Naoom.

As he danced, his breast pocket was stuffed with the yield of his search on the previous day. His dirty face, despite its stupid look, was bursting with good health. Suddenly, he stopped dancing and rushed toward the street. Our neighbor, Umm Shukri, said, "I bet he just heard the singing of the gypsies and so ran to them. He indeed lacks nothing but a gypsy girl to whom they should marry him!"

On hearing that, I dashed running to follow him. But my mother saw me and shouted at me before I even reached the outside gate of the courtyard, and she ordered me to come back immediately. The stern tone of voice made me understand she was very serious. And I returned.

 **10**

In the year 1927, an earthquake in Palestine terrified the people. It was most devastating in the city of Nablus, where many houses collapsed as a result and there were numerous victims.

In Bethlehem countless houses were destroyed too, especially the dilapidated ones, and many others were cracked. The earth split open in different places and caused much fear. The inhabitants prayed every day in the morning and the evening, hoping God would forgive them and spare them His severity and wrath.*

Following that, Patriarch Elias III came to Bethlehem from his headquarters in Mardin, Turkey (later moved to Hims, Syria) in order to inspect the state of his flock. His coming to

---

*This earthquake was a frightening experience. I have described some of its effects in chapter 6 of my novel, *In Search of Walleed Masoud,* which will make me dispense with repetition here.

us was like the coming of a messenger from Heaven, for his round and bearded face shone with a strange goodness. He visited us at school with all his awe-inspiring dignity, wearing his black and crimson clerical garments, his head covered with a shining black miter and his chest adorned with a magnificent necklace from which a large cross studded with red and blue precious stones was suspended. He spoke to us baffled little urchins about the one nature of Christ, and he rejected the claims of "the heretics who distorted the teachings of the early Fathers by saying Christ had two natures." As I listened to his beautiful, velvety voice, I imagined that I began to understand matters of great importance, however difficult they were for my boyish mind.

We were told afterward that the patriarch himself would celebrate the divine liturgy in the morning of the following day, which happened to be a Sunday, and that he would give "an apostolic sermon" in the service. Everyone began to look forward to hearing it with great expectation.

At dawn the following day, my father got up and awakened my brother and me in order for us to prepare ourselves to attend the divine liturgy and serve in it. As usual, the three of us left before sunrise without eating and headed for the church. The candles had not yet been lit, so we helped the sexton to light them. The priests, the deacons, and the choir members arrived, and the church began to fill with worshipers. Then the patriarch came, surrounded by monks and bishops, and he sat on a carved gilt chair which was like a throne and which had been especially brought for him that morning and placed in front of the iconostas separating the altar from the rest of the church. On the iconostas there was an image of Christ crucified, with angels carrying cups to receive the blood flowing from his pierced hands as a Roman soldier on horseback stabbed his side with a spear and blood gushed from the wound. The two choirs began to sing hymns, and the singers, including my brother and me, began to recite from the large hand-written volumes placed on the two lecterns in front of the altar, one on the right and the other on the left.

After more than two hours of hymns, readings, and prayers, the rituals of the divine liturgy began. We went behind the altar and put on the robes of singers. The patriarch put on his resplendent, brocaded vestments and the priests their beautiful, colored cloaks. The curtain was pulled aside to reveal the altar which we, who served the liturgy, stood before in two parallel lines. Meanwhile, the great pontiff began to perform his ritual duties with the help of the priests, the singers, and the censer carriers.

The church was crowded to capacity, and most of the humble worshipers carried lit candles, whose smoke filled the air. I had been standing up for approximately four hours when the time for the sermon arrived. I began feeling unusually tired, and I tried to ignore a terrible colic in my stomach because I wanted to hear the sermon and listen attentively to every word of it. His Beatitude the Patriarch moved to the middle lectern, which held a large manuscript of the Gospel bound in silver covers, on which were carved scenes from the life of Jesus Christ.

For an unknown reason, two of my friends and I were asked to stand, with candles in our hands, in front of this lectern. At that moment, the patriarch raised his left hand holding the staff topped by a carving of Prophet Moses' serpent that revived all those looking at it, and he moved his right hand holding a large cross with a beautiful handkerchief at its base, and he made the sign of the cross in the air saying in a resonant, loud voice, "In the name of the Father, the Son, and the Holy Spirit." Suddenly, my interior writhed with pain and a long moan came from my throat, as I saw myself fall to the ground against my will—and I passed out.

It seems that my sudden fall in front of the patriarch, with all the worshipers' eyes on the venerable preacher who was seen as a saint from the old days, caused some confusion in the congregation. A group of men rushed to me, and one of them picked me up before my father did and raised me to his chest. They then took me out into the fresh air.

When I came to, I found I was being carried by a man I did

not know, and in the din of people around, I was being taken upstairs, unconscious of what was happening. They brought me into the Society's hall and laid me down on a sofa. By that time, I had regained some consciousness, so I sat up. But before I could say anything, my stomach contracted, and I threw up its small contents on the floor. As they cleaned the tiles, one man asked, "What have you eaten this morning, boy?"

"Nothing . . . nothing at all," I muttered.

Suddenly I remembered that, when I was hungry the night before, I had eaten several green and yellow cucumbers without peeling them, and then I went to bed without eating anything else. The result was what had happened that morning.

Reassured by my condition, the men returned to church to listen to the rest of the sermon. My father carried me in his arms despite my remonstration and took me downstairs as the patriarch's voice, strong and charming, reached our ears from the open church door.

That tempted my father to stop for a moment or two at the door as the voice conveyed strange words which I listened to, my chest resting on my father's: "And as St. Ephrem said in his epistle to the ascetics of Edessa: 'Hold fast to faith and prayer and be like Christ in the wilderness, fearing neither hunger nor wild beasts, and you shall not be polluted by sin, for you have thrown off the yoke of this world and the tyranny of possessions.'"

As these words were being spoken, my father hastened to the road with me, and I asked him, "What is the meaning of the tyranny of possessions?"

He said, "By God, Son, I haven't understood a single word . . . you have frightened me and made me miss a wonderful sermon."

At home my mother said as she was busy preparing lunch, "But why don't you ever eat something before going to the divine liturgy?"

"God forbid!" exclaimed my father. "Do you want us to behave like Catholics, who eat breakfast and are full, then sway along to church at nine o'clock when the sun is high in the fore-noon sky? Don't you know that God, may He be praised and exalted, accepts the prayer of only those who are hungry or fasting?"

And my mother agreed, "By God, you are right, Ibrahim."

∎ ∎ ∎

We moved to another house. At first I did not know why my parents decided on moving from time to time. But I later understood that rent was the most important factor, if the new rent was lower than the previous one, an additional factor being perhaps the space of the house. From *al-khashashi* (the huts), we moved to a home in the Dabdoub Close; and after a short period, we moved again to Fathu's house. A man named Fathallah had rented an old, two-story house, of which he occupied the upper floor. He sublet the lower floor to us, access to which was gained by descending a flight of stairs conforming to the natural incline of the ground and leading to a large green plot which the door to our home opened onto. We spent two exhausting days moving our household effects and bedding to the new house, carrying them on our heads and backs and helped by some friends and neighbors. Our new residence consisted of a somewhat large room, separated from the sheep fold and the chicken coop by a wooden partition. The chickens had a small opening in the outside wall, level with one of the steps of the stairs, through which they entered and left at will. As for the sheep, we had to bring them in through our room, take them to their fold, then close the door in the wooden partition. Bedbugs infested this wooden partition in dreadful abundance, and we could not put an end to them despite great efforts; they invaded our beds on hot nights and sucked our blood with spiteful persistence.

But this home had certain advantages. Since it was in the lower floor of the building, its ceiling was vaulted, and thus it was protected by the room above it from leakage and seepage in the rainy season. Furthermore, in the corner of the ceiling there was a square opening with a trapdoor, connecting us directly—when opened—with the upper room and permitting us to speak or communicate with the Fathu family, which was especially convenient after Sulayman, Fathallah's youngest son, became one of my dearest friends.

In addition, this residence opened directly on the area overlooking the New Road, the valley next to it, and the hills beyond. And so we could see the distant horizon, beginning with the heights to the north and ending in the east with the blue mountains which the sun rose behind. The heights were topped by Ramat Rahel and St. Elias monastery with its distinctive dome and concealed the city of Jerusalem.

This endless opening to the world was the source of great pleasure to me: we saw sunrise with its vivid colors every day, and we saw a glow of light every night all along the northern horizon as we sat on the stone stairs for our evening gathering. When I asked my brother Yusuf about the strange light, he said without hesitation, "It is the light of the city of Jerusalem. God wants it to glow in the midst of the darkness that fills the world."

There were two large almond trees on the edge of the alley leading down to our home. We shared their fruit with the neighbors when it was still green. More importantly, I climbed them and felt in the middle of that vast space that I was on top of the world. My imagination wandered in the direction of the distant horizons supporting the heavens, and I wished I could reach them, climb to their summits, open an aperture in the sky, and enter from it to where I would see God and the angels.

But there was a small unpleasant problem, which my brother Yusuf and I had to deal with whenever we returned home late after dark. At the beginning of the dirt road leading from the main road down to our home, there was a huge fig tree with intertwined branches that we had to pass by. We were told that an old demon lived under it or in its branches. What was the story of this demon? They said that a man was killed one night under this tree by being stabbed with knives. His blood flowed on the ground and was absorbed by the earth. A few days passed before someone came by, recognized the dead man, and carried him to his relatives. They did not know who killed him, and no one ever avenged him. That is why a demon arose from his spilled blood and woke up at night, waylaid those passing under the tree or near it, and asked them to take vengeance on the killer, if he did not choke them in a fit of anger. So when we returned home in the dark, we were terrified on reaching the fig tree lest he should come out to us; we passed as fast as we could, making the sign of the cross repeatedly because demons—like devils—were afraid of the sign of the cross, for it petrified them and rendered them harmless.

My friend George's house was near ours and next to that of Khalil Zmairiyya, the owner of most of the larger green terraced plots surrounding us and which abounded in pomegranate, mulberry, and fig trees. Khalil was a craftsman who made mother-of-pearl crosses and rosaries at home with his wife, which the souvenir shops on Manger Square sold on his behalf. He often invited George, Sulayman, and me to sit down on the ground in his workshop and help him by making holes in beads or rubbing the back of the little crosses with a blue waxy material, which caused the word *Bethlehem* or *Jerusalem* to appear in Latin characters that he engraved with surprising speed. In return, he permitted us to play in his green terraced plots, even in the season of pomegranates, mulberries, and figs. But if we brought friends with us and were too rough with the trees, he came suddenly upon us, shouting and carrying his whip. We took to our heels, and he ran behind us, heaping loud curses on us and cracking his whip in the air. Two or three days later, he forgave us, forgot what had happened, and invited us again to help him in his daily work.

The large green terraced plot, onto which the door of our house opened, was much below the level of the house. Because crossing it shortened the distance to the New Road, from which we descended into the Jamal Valley and the olive groves in our constant search for wildflowers and plants, grasshoppers and cicadas, snails and lizards, it became our custom to leap into the terraced plot without bothering to arrange four or five stones like steps to facilitate our descent. In our play, we were always on the go. We jumped, ran, and climbed in bare feet. We also played football barefoot.

One morning I leapt into the terraced plot to follow my friends, and my right foot landed squarely on the bottom of a broken glass bottle, which appeared as though it had been specially set up for me there like a trap. The vicious glass bottle almost split the sole of my foot. I collapsed in a heap on the earth and stones; then I managed to drag my bleeding foot and climb up the wall as best I could, and return home weeping. My mother hastened to attend to me, rebuking me for my ceaseless horsing around. After mopping up the blood, she treated the deep wound in the usual manner with cobwebs— that is, with spider web which, thank God, was plentiful around the house. I lay on the mat for three days, which would have been as bad as hell, if I had not played with my little brother, Issa, and our favorite cat, Fulla. After that, I bandaged my foot with a rag, and, notwithstanding the pain and the warnings of my mother and grandmother, I returned to jumping and running with my friends. And I returned to school.

As I passed by the haunted fig tree, it occurred to me that its demon had something to do with what had happened to me. The cursed demon spilled my blood, and he had no more right to harm me! I said so to my brother Yusuf, and he laughed and said, "What has the demon to do with you? You are innocent, and the demon still awaits the real criminal."

I asked him, "Why then are you also afraid when passing by the fig tree at night?"

He shook his head and said, "I don't know. We should not be afraid. You and I . . . will not be afraid as of tonight! Agreed?"

"Agreed," I said. "We will not be afraid!"

■ ■ ■

At the house of Khalil Zmairiyya, George and I were helping Uncle Khalil to string the beads of rosaries, when George's father passed by to inform us that a group of boys, a little older than we were, were preparing themselves to go to Jerusalem in the company of Teacher Jiryis to be ordained deacons by Bishop Mikhail at St. Mark's Convent on the following morning. He said to his son, "Why don't you, too, go with them, spend the night at your aunt's in Jerusalem, and come back tomorrow after the service?"

George looked at me and asked, "What do you think? Will you come with me?"

I said, "I'll ask my mother first."

I ran home to tell my mother that I was going to Jerusalem for the ordination service at the convent and that I would spend the night with George at his aunt's house. But my mother did not approve of this whim.

"How are you going to Jerusalem?"

"On foot."

"And how are you returning?"

"On foot."

"No. You're not going."

However, despite her rejection, the tone of her voice was not resolute as it usually was when she was serious. She went back to her chores without reiterating her refusal. Moments later, George came along, having put on his shoes; so I put on my shoes. That day, my mother had roasted a quantity of salted watermelon seeds, as was her custom on most Saturdays. So I filled one of my jacket pockets with seeds. We knew that the boys heading for Jerusalem would take the road which our house commanded a view of.

We did not wait long near the two almond trees; we saw the teacher, tall and walking fast with four boys. I yelled to my mother, "Mom! I'm going to Jerusalem with the group!" George and I leapt into the terraced plot and from it to the road, and we joined them. I was filled with an extraordinary impetuosity because I was about to see Jerusalem with my friends. I had seen it only once before when my mother took me in order to buy me a pair of shoes that I hated and wanted to forget.

How wonderful it was that afternoon to go beyond Rachel's Dome and reach the large carob tree on the left side of the road—that lone tree, exploding from the earth among the dusty olive trees like a vast green dome, to whose cool shade under the dense branches and leaves we often resorted whenever we went far from home on hot summer days in search of grapes on vines. It was our favorite station on our trip to and from St. Elias Convent, the convent being until that time the farthest place I ever went to on foot in the direction of Jerusalem.

Passing by the beautiful carob tree, the gate of the old convent, and its abandoned well, we continued our way to Lower Baqaa and hence to Tori. As we began descending the hill toward the Sultan's Pool, the ramparts of the Old City and the minaret of David the Prophet became visible to us, bathed as they were in the violet twilight of the setting sun. We then climbed up toward Jaffa Gate.

We knew that the distance was eight kilometers from the marker stones on both sides of the road—those oblong stones on which were carved the numbers of kilometers and which I liked to sit on for a little while whenever I reached one of them, proud of the distance I had walked. Many years afterward, I was to take that road back and forth dozens of times so that I would come to know all its stone quarries, each rock on the wayside, each olive tree and vine, each house looking out onto it—the houses then were few—and I would come to know each door and each window, their forms and their colors.

The sun had set completely when we entered the Jaffa Gate market and came down its wide and smooth stone steps as the shops on both sides had begun to light their lanterns. When we reached the first arch where the road branched, one road rising as it turned right toward the convent, the other going left toward the Christian Quarter, and a third continuing forward to Khan al-Zayt and the Holy Sanctuary (of the Dome of the Rock and the Aqsa Mosque), we left the group with the understanding that we would rejoin them at the convent next morning. George and I climbed a few stairs and turned into a narrow alley. The houses were huddled together, their windows squatting on the doors and their stairs clinging to the alley corners. Faint lights lit up small squares here and there, increasing the density of the dark in the unlit areas. Excited and anxious at the same time, I felt a delightful pleasure mixed with fear.

I said to my friend, "Do you know the way to your aunt's house? Are you sure?"

He dragged me by the arm, taking me under a low arch to another alley, and he said, "Not only in the daytime, but at night, too."

A little later, we were in a courtyard surrounded by several open doors, and children and women were all over the place. George rushed to an old woman who was lighting a kerosene lamp at that moment, and he shouted, "Auntie! Auntie!"

Overjoyed by the surprise, she turned to him and received him in her arms. He introduced me to her, and she welcomed us profusely. She spread out a thin mat on the floor and made us sit on it, and she brought a watermelon on a copper tray and placed it in front of us. She then brought a knife and cut the watermelon, saying, "Lord, let it be red!" And it was red and delicious, with very black seeds. We were exhausted after our long journey on foot, and so the watermelon was the most delightful thing in the world to see, smell, and touch. When George's aunt brought us bread and Nablus cheese, and when we divided the watermelon into segments, she said as I contemplated the wrinkles on her kind face, "Come on, sweethearts, eat. Afterward, tell me about what brought you here today. . . ."

■ ■ ■

The sun had not risen when Auntie Umm Yaqoub woke us up. She said, "Don't be noisy; Yaqoub is asleep and will not go to the service. I've prepared some tea, olives, and cheese for you. Have your breakfast and then go to the convent. The liturgy is going to be very long."

We had slept in our clothes, only taking off our shoes. We put them on while Yaqoub (it became evident he was at least thirty years old) was lying on his back, fast asleep with his mouth open. We took our breakfast and went on our way to the convent as Auntie said good-bye and promised, "I'll see you there later."

At the convent, I was fascinated by the altar of the church adorned with gilt engravings, and by its huge candle stands, its twinkling oil lamps, and its three or four paintings hanging high on the walls and enchanting my eyes raised up to them willy-nilly. I took part in serving the liturgy, though I was in fact completely lost in the crowd of chanters, deacons, and monks who were by far more adept at singing and praying than I and my friends were.

Then came the turn of ordination, and I did not understand anything of it save that it meant "the placing of hands," which has continued in succession from Christ the Lord to Peter the Apostle, and thence through the church fathers for almost two thousand years to this day. The bishop, then, was to put his hand on my head and connect me with the blessing of Jesus Christ himself.

The bishop cut a lock of my hair and prayed in Syriac while the tips of his fingers were on my head, then he attired me with a sash over my singer's robe in a manner formally symbolizing the first of the ordination ranks, while I hardly believed my eyes. I thought I was in an impossible dream.

Finally the worshipers went outdoors. I took off my white robe and my sash in the vestiary next to the altar and wandered among the worshipers in the open courtyard. I climbed a flight of stairs to the upper floor, spurred on by my curiosity, and I roamed about in the aimlessly scrambling chaos of the old building, remembering that Christ had his Last Supper in one of its rooms before he was betrayed and crucified. I saw monks withdrawing to their cells, but no one paid any attention to me. When I went downstairs to the courtyard, I could not find any of my group. Even George had disappeared. I went out to the alleys I did not know, full of fear and confusion mitigated only by my joy at seeing the ever-winding and ever-ramifying roads going up and down, filled with children in their Sunday clothes. I realized that I would never find the way to the house of my friend's aunt in those paths, however hard I tried.

I suddenly found I was in the Little Market (*al-Suwayqa*) with all its hustle and bustle. I climbed its smooth steps leading to Jaffa Gate and decided to go down to the nearby square where cars and carriages were parking, waiting for passengers going to Bethlehem and Hebron.

A seller of licorice drink passed by me, carrying a large jar on his chest covered with a long, red wrap. He had fixed a big piece of ice on the mouth of the jar, and was beautifully jingling two brass plates in his left hand in a repetitive rhythm. Around his waist was a belt with a rack on which several brass cups were arranged, and he repeated his melodic call saying, "Cold licorice drink!" As a buyer stood in front of him, the licorice seller took a cup from his belt with his right hand and gracefully bent his body a little and poured a thin stream of brown liquid from of the metal spout of the jar into the cup until it over-flowed with a foamy head.

It was a delectable scene, which I could only enjoy visually. I walked among the cars and carriages, looking at the drivers with some anxiety and hoping one of them would recognize me. But who in the city would recognize a stranger who is a child eight years old and has nothing in his pocket but a few watermelon seeds?

I raised my hand to my head and touched the place from which the bishop had cut a lock of my hair: would the blessing of heaven perhaps descend upon me through the empty space left by the lost lock?

I had no choice but to go back home on foot. "Let me start my long journey," I thought. I had been on my feet since sunrise, and a large black clock I saw above one of the shops in the Jaffa Gate area indicated it was eleven o'clock.

I hurried up in order to forget I was tired, the first part of the road being a downward slope. I was facing the sun, but I did not care. I would go back to my family and tell them about Jerusalem and my ordination. The road stretched before me, and the distance between milestones seemed very long. . . . I was sweating, and became thirsty and hungry. I was exhausted. I scrutinized every car or carriage driver passing by me, hoping I would recognize him or he would me, to no avail. I reached the four-kilometer marker. I sat on a rock to rest, then I resumed my walking.

I was about to reach the five-kilometer marker. I had des-paired of being saved. The sun was beating on my head, and I no longer looked up at any car or carriage passing by. All of a sudden, a fast car that had passed me stopped abruptly, backed up, and stopped by me. The driver shouted, "Where are you going in this sweltering heat, boy? What brings you on this road?"

I immediately recognized him. He was Abu Naeem, a tall burly man who always leaned on a thick stick when walking and gestured with it when talking, adding awesomeness and conviction to his loud words. His son Naeem was one of my schoolmates, we were even classmates, and I had often gone to their house and he to ours.

"I am coming from Jerusalem and going home," I said.

"Come on," he commanded. "Get in the car."

The car was full of passengers.

"How can I?" I asked.

He said, "Come, sit beside me, between me and this gentleman, although it is forbidden to take extra passengers . . . but we'll see; it can be arranged."

The man next to him opened the car door. I got in and squeezed myself by him and sat next to the driver on the comfortable leather seat on which his thick stick leaned.

I said, "But you see, Uncle, I don't have a single piaster."

Abu Naeem laughed, stroked my cheek, and joked, "You bastard, did I ask you for any money? But look, if we spot a policeman on the way, you will have to duck down and hide underfoot. Understand? Let's go."

He asked me about my father, and I told him about what I had done that morning. He was surprised that his son Naeem had not come with us to the ordination liturgy, but nobody had told him about it. The car was very comfortable, although I had to gather myself up in a small space and I could smell the odor of gasoline. We reached Bethlehem without being seen by the traffic police. I got out at the beginning of Ras Iftays street and ran home. My family were about to sit down and have their Sunday dinner. My father said, "I told them I would not eat a single morsel until you came. I was looking for you on the road, expecting to see you. How have you returned? Tell us, what did you do?"

I said, "In a moment. Let me first take off these cursed shoes."

■ ■ ■

After dinner, I ran to George's house to learn what had happened to him. His mother told me he was at the neighbors', at Khalil Zmairiyya's. I went there, and as soon as he saw me at the door, he came out to me and joyfully asked, "My aunt took me to the car and paid my fare. Where have you been? We looked for you everywhere. Come in, join Uncle Khalil."

When I entered, I saw a young man wearing a hat and a suit of a strange cut. He said he had returned from Chile to see his family after a long absence. His name was Miquel, and he was Uncle Khalil's brother-in-law. This young man was extremely nice to us and began to tell us about his life in Santiago, mixing his Arabic with Spanish words so that we could hardly understand him. But we understood that he was famous for his strength. He suddenly took off his jacket, rolled up his sleeves, and showed us his muscles bulging like smooth rock. He then said to me, "Do you have a piaster coin?"

I said, "Not even a half-piaster."

He said, "That's fine, I have one."

He took out a round coin from his pocket, gave it to me and said, "Can you bend it between your fingers?"

I said, "This is iron. How can I bend it?"

He said, "Give it to me; I'll show you."

He placed it between his thumb and his forefinger, and he bent it as if it were a piece of paper. He then took an iron bar, which Khalil Zmairiyya used in his work, and he held it in his hands by its ends and bent it in half with his amazing might, while Uncle Khalil was shouting, "No, Miquel! I have no other bar! No, Miquel!"

Proud of his strength, he smiled confidently and said, "Well, then. Here!" And he pushed the ends apart until the bar became straight in his hands.

He amazed us with his strength, and on the next day, we

brought him a number of metallic bottle caps that we had collected from the street and asked him to bend them. Without laughing or smiling, he took three or four of them, bent them all, and threw them away. He spoke little, and his face was always downcast for some unknown reason.

When I returned to see him a few days later, I found Uncle Khalil in a state of intense agitation, his wife was weeping and lamenting, and it seemed she had been crying continuously for many hours. I went to George's house, and his mother informed me that Miquel had gone the previous night to the Bethlehem Young Men's Club, where he took one of the members to one side, then stabbed him repeatedly with a knife until he collapsed in a pool of blood, and "fluttered like a slain bird." Miquel then left the club to return home, but the police arrested him on the way and detained him at the police station on Manger Square, where he was imprisoned.

I remembered the demon who frightened us at night by his appearance from under the fig tree, which was no more than fifty steps away from the place we were, and I asked her, "Has Miquel taken vengeance for the murder of a member of his family?"

George's mother replied, "I don't know. But, poor guy! They say he is going to be hanged."

The Young Men's Club was not far from the places George and I frequented with our friends: it was just behind the Church of the Nativity. That is why, before going to school on the next day, we both hastened to the club and stood at the door, opposite the press of Issa al-Bandak's newspaper, *Sawt al-Shaab* (*The Voice of the People*). The door was open and unattended for some reason. After some hesitation, we stepped over the threshold, and in a corner next to the entrance, we saw a terrifying pool of dark, dry blood and stains soiling a large area of the floor and the walls, indicating the violent tremors the stabbed man must have had.

We immediately withdrew, shuddering. I imagined Miquel with his steel-hard muscles as he stabbed the victim repeatedly, and I pictured the latter as he struggled in his own blood on the floor. My shudder redoubled, and I felt my innards turning.

Dumbfounded, George uttered, "He was strong. . . ."

I said, "Yes. Very strong. . . ."

As we headed for school, we said nothing more to each other. That day, I understood nothing of my lessons, for the pool of blood and the stains never left my imagination. Did Miquel come from the other end of the world, from Chile, in order to implement the will of the demon living in our fig tree and take revenge? Or would another demon now rise from the blood spilled in the club to waylay passersby at night and demand a new vengeance?

Every time I later passed by the club door, that tragic vision and that feeling of terror returned to me. I had not seen what happened, but the pool of blood I had seen that morning convinced me that I had witnessed the killing. I wished I had never seen it. I did not know that that pool, a few years later, was to become larger and larger until it engulfed the whole world.

11

Once upon a time, a long, long time ago, a hermit named Malik lived in our country.

This hermit left all the joys and pleasures of the world and went far away from the city. He settled in a mountain cave and lived on a small quantity of bread, dates, and water, which he brought from the nearest village each week.

In that cave, he fasted and prayed from morning to evening. He praised God repeatedly and sought His forgiveness and favor. Days passed, and he did not stop praising God and praying to Him.

One night, having dispelled all seductive apparitions by increasing his prayers and continually beating his chest with a stone whenever he suspected Satan was whispering to him, he felt he must have satisfied his Lord with his ascetic life and his piety. He lit a candle, and it illuminated the ragged rock, and the strange plants suspended from it, before which he knelt.

He fixed the candle in a crack in the rock and said, "Lord! Lord!"

He waited for a while, but God did not answer him. He thought to himself that God had not heard him because of His many preoccupations with human beings, both the good ones and the evil ones. He therefore repeated his call, but in a louder voice this time, "Lord! Lord!"

When no answer came, he beat his chest with the stone and gave a great shout that shook the cave saying, "O Lord! O Lord!"

And lo, the candle flickered as though a great wind had blown, and it was about to be extinguished. But it recovered its flame, and its light became as bright as a raging fire when a thundering voice said, "Malik! My beloved hermit, Malik! Have you called me?"

The hermit prostrated himself and said as his head was on the ground, "Lord! Are You satisfied with me? Have I done my duty as You wish?"

The voice said, "I am satisfied, but only to a certain extent. For, a few miles away, there is one who is more worthy of my satisfaction than you."

"Another hermit, my God?"

The voice was tender this time, "No, Malik, a poor man. His name is Ibrahim, and he makes millstones. Go and ask about him."

"I will, Lord; I will in order to learn how to please You."

Next morning, Malik took his staff and left the cave. He descended to the village and asked there about Ibrahim, the maker of millstones. Having been shown the place, he found a man sitting on the ground near a ruined hut, in the shade of old bags which he had spread on dry branches firmly fixed in the wall of the hut to form a roof to protect him like an umbrella from the heat of the sun. In front of him was an almost round stone he was working on with his chisel and hammer to make one of the two parts of a hand mill.

The hermit greeted him. Interrupting his work, the man raised his eyes from the stone and graciously returned the greeting. He looked up at that disheveled man standing before him, leaning on a long staff. When the visitor said nothing, the man asked, "Do you want to buy a millstone?"

The hermit said, "I have nothing to do with millstones. I've come to visit you."

Ibrahim immediately called his wife, and she came running out to him. He said to her, "Bring some food for our honored guest to eat."

The hermit said, "No, I only need a drink of water."

As the woman brought what he needed, the hermit sat on a stone near the shed and asked the man sitting among the stone chips, "What will you do with this millstone, Ibrahim?"

"Every two or three days, I finish a grinder consisting of two millstones and a handle. I then carry it to the city, and I sell it."

"And then?"

"I sell it for four dirhams, of which I give two to the poor. I then buy food and other necessities for my wife and myself with the remaining two dirhams."

"Is this all that you do?"

"I wish I could do more. Whenever I see hungry people, I say I should make more grinders and sell more of them for their sake. But the Lord, in His wisdom, has given me two hands only."

The hermit got up and said as he was about to leave, "God bless you. You are a virtuous man."

Ibrahim stood up and asked, "What is your name, venerable hermit?"

"My name is Malik, and I've come to learn from you."

"How can someone like you learn anything from me? God, forgive me. . . . Listen, we have four chickens, three of which lay eggs. Take one of them; what do you think?"

When the hermit declined the offer, Ibrahim insisted and said, "We have gathered six or seven eggs. Take them to your cell; you may need them." And he asked his wife to bring the eggs. But Malik refused to take them and thanked him, claiming that he had to go to the city on an urgent errand and that carrying eggs was troublesome.

Ibrahim said, "Are you going to the city just like that,

without shoes, reverend father? By God, I shall not let you go before you try on my shoes; they may fit you." He ran to his hut and came back with a pair of shoes that were in good condition.

The hermit was surprised at all this and said, "But these are your own shoes!"

"Why not? You need them more than I do now, and you have no source of income. I have these stones which I transform into millstones, and I buy my necessities with the income from selling them."

Malik turned around to leave hurriedly, saying, "Good-bye, my pious and generous friend."

He returned to his cave, having realized that his conceit would have degraded him in the sight of the Lord if he had continued to believe he was the best and most pious of men. And he decided to speak once more to his Lord that evening.

At night, he lit his candle, knelt down, and prayed fervently. Repentant and humble, he then raised his voice and said, "Lord! Lord!"

This time, the response came quickly, "What do you want, Malik?"

He began beating his chest with his fists, "I ask Your forgiveness and pardon, Lord! Forgive my suspicions and transgressions. . . . I have visited Your servant Ibrahim and found him, as You said, a man whose virtue and piety I can never emulate."

The voice said, "Your sins are forgiven, so long as you appreciate the virtue and piety of others."

Malik thereupon raised his head as he contemplated the abundant light shed by the little candle on the rocks before him, and he said, "But, my Lord, why do You keep a man like Ibrahim poor? Why don't You bestow greater wealth on him so that it may spread to others, too?"

The voice answered, "Malik, do you want to take Ibrahim away from Me? Don't you see that he is a faithful and pious man whose loss I might fear?"

But the hermit was resolved to argue with his Lord after what he had seen that morning. He said, "Lord, You have often given generously to evil men, and they have not hesitated to disobey You and reject Your love. Why don't You also give to this good man, who has spent his life seeking Your love and obeying You?"

"Malik, you make Me fear for what might happen to him."

"I will be responsible for him, Lord."

"You will make Me lose him."

"On the contrary. You will see, he will become closer to You."

"Malik. . . ."

"Try him, my Lord. And try me with him."

"You will make Me lose him. However, I will grant this strange and persistent request of yours."

"What do You want me to tell him, Lord?"

"Go tomorrow and tell him to take fifty-one steps from the back of his hut in the direction of the leaning fig tree, where he will see a moss-covered rock. Let him dig a pit there as deep as a man's height, and he will find a treasure which nobody will share with him. . . . Are you satisfied now? And don't you speak to me again until a year or more has passed. . . ."

"Lord! How great You are!"

The voice finally said in a somewhat displeased tone, "Enough, enough! But if Ibrahim abandons Me, if I lose him, I shall consign him to hellfire, and I shall put you there with him! Keep this in mind!"

On the next day, the hermit did what God had commanded him, and he stayed with the maker of millstones as he took the fifty-one steps and then dug all day by the moss-covered rock until his ax hit an iron box. As soon as Ibrahim broke its cover, he saw gold coins, diamond and pearl necklaces, and precious stones of all sizes and colors heaped up in it in a disorderly manner.

The sun had set when Ibrahim and his wife started to bring the box out of the deep pit with the help of the hermit. The process was not easy, because the box was big and heavy and the hours of night were passing quickly. It was almost dawn when they finally succeeded in raising the box to the surface and carrying it to the hut.

Ibrahim took a handful of that shining treasure and gave it to Malik saying, "Here, take this. It is yours, Malik. . . ." But Malik refused to touch it. He began rather to shake the soil from his tattered, black frock and the dirt that had clung to his beard, and he said, "All I want is a bowl of water. I am very thirsty."

He drank the water, embraced his beloved friend, wished him well, then took his staff and left him with his wife in God's protection. He returned to his cave, exhausted but fully satisfied with what he had done. He thanked God and praised Him; then he lay on the rocks and slept soundly.

Days passed, and in stories, they pass like the winds and like dreams. Malik was certain that Ibrahim would not disappoint him in doing good deeds. So he resolved not to interfere and to remain far from worldly affairs, continuing his fasting and praying to please his Lord; perhaps He would answer him when he talked to Him again. . . .

Spring and summer passed, then the fall. Winter came, harsh as usual and full of storms and rains. When it ended, it ushered in a beautiful spring, and grass covered the slopes of the mountain. Summer arrived once again, and Malik thought of going down to see his beloved friend Ibrahim and learning what abundant benefits he had bestowed on people from what God had given him.

He descended to the village, seeking the hut he knew. He found it to be the ruin it had been, and next to it were the torn bags spread on the dry branches, forming a roof under which were a few abandoned pieces of rock. He knocked on the old door, not expecting an answer. But he was surprised to see Ibrahim's wife come out to him, disheveled, pale, and tattered.

He asked her about what happened, and she said, "You're asking me about what happened? He left me and has not come back to me. . . . Go to the city and ask about your friend Ibrahim's palace there, then ask him (rather than me) about what happened. . . ."

Malik was greatly troubled, and he hurried to the city, where he began to ask people about the palace of Ibrahim, the millstone maker. They pointed it out to him in the suburb: it was a large house which had three floors and stood in the middle of a garden with tall fruit-laden trees, and it was surrounded by a high fence made of black-painted iron bars, the tops of which were painted gold.

He went to the big closed gate and shook it. From a side room, a burly man came out carrying a whip in his hand and wearing a brocaded shirt and trousers woven of gold thread. He asked the hermit through the bars of the closed gate, "What do you want?"

The hermit said, "I want to see my friend Ibrahim."

The man gave him a look of scorn mixed with surprise, "Did you say you wanted to see Ibrahim Bey?"

He answered in all simplicity, "Yes. Tell him, 'Your friend Malik is at the door.' You'll see, he will come to me immediately."

The gatekeeper crackled his whip twice, and a servant came running to him. He whispered something in his ear, and the servant hurried into the house. A moment later, he returned and whispered in the gatekeeper's ear while Malik was holding the bars of the closed gate. The gatekeeper said, "Ibrahim Bey says he does not know anyone named Malik. Please, go away."

"But I am his friend, and I must see him."

The gatekeeper opened a small door in the big gate and came out to him threatening him with his whip, "Are you going to leave or shall I work your back over with this?"

"Beat me as you like. I shall not move an inch from here until I see him."

The gatekeeper whipped the hermit on the back and kicked his buttocks as one would a dog, and he said, "Get going, beggar. The Bey's guests will soon arrive and he will be angry to know they saw a barefoot man at his door with your looks, your tatters, and your staff. . . ." And he gave him another stinging blow with his whip.

Malik withdrew a few steps, moaning. He sat on a rock in full view of the house and said, "I'll stay here until the millstone maker comes out to me."

Men and women of all kinds began to arrive on beautiful

horses or in shining carriages. Doors were opened wide for them, and music and singing could be heard from inside the house. . . . Whenever Malik tried to steal in with some of them as they entered, more than one doorkeeper and guard pushed him back, beat him, and threw him back to his rock.

The day passed, then the night. Before dawn, the celebrating guests came out, drunk and staggering, and they mounted their horses and took their carriages. They left while Malik remained huddled on his rock, hungry and thirsty, but determined to stay and do what he had resolved to do. The house became quiet, and the lights were extinguished.

Malik got up, went close to one side of the fence, and before any one of the palace guards was aware of him, shouted in the direction of the windows with all the power to shout left in him, "Ibrahim! Ibrahim! O millstone maker!"

After repeating his shout a few times, one of the windows was opened, and he saw a person he recognized as his old friend, so he shouted to him, "I am Malik, O Ibrahim. I have come to see you."

The response was the window closing with a bang.

Moments later, the burly gatekeeper came out to him, took away his staff, and broke it into two pieces. He then whipped his back with stinging blows, and kicked and shoved him. . . . Finally the hermit fell face downward, his beard sullied with dirt, and broke into sobs.

He then stood up and went away, beating his chest as tears ran down his cheeks and beard. He did not reach his cave until sunset and after a long tedious journey. Exhausted, he flung himself on the floor, drank a little water, and ate a piece of bread and a few hard dates as he continued to beat his chest and lament.

He lit the candle, knelt down, and prayed. Supplicating God, he shouted while on his knees, "Lord, Lord! If You are still willing to hear me, answer me, Lord!"

The candle light brightened, and he heard the thundering voice, which he had not heard for many months, "Malik! Malik! What have you done with the man I loved?"

He said as tears choked his imploring voice, "Lord, have mercy on me! I have consigned him to hellfire and myself with him! Sinner that I am, ignorant and stupid, I have disobeyed You and argued against Your wisdom and will."

The voice came to him saying, "It is difficult for Me to see you burn in hellfire after all the suffering you have gone through."

"But, Lord, I guaranteed him, and I deserve Your punishment."

"Your weeping and your lamentation have saddened Me, O Malik. . . . What you have suffered is enough, and don't you ever go again to his palace. Leave him to Me and devote yourself to your fasting and prayers."

Once more in our story, days passed quickly like the winds and like dreams. But they passed like nightmares for Ibrahim. His sheep and cattle were afflicted with an epidemic two days later, and they all died after one week. One week later, the ships carrying his commercial goods sank. Two weeks later, the big firm he had established was bankrupt, and debtors came to him from every direction. He did not have enough money to pay the salaries of his employees and the wages of his servants and maids. One after another, they all abandoned him, and so did his friends—his companions of fun and play as well as his mistresses. He mortgaged his palace, but the mortgage was foreclosed soon afterward. The summer months were hardly gone when he found himself chased out, homeless on the open road, penniless and dispossessed, with no one to greet him and say, "Good morning." The Lord giveth and the Lord taketh.

The autumn winds blew on the ruined hut, and as Ibrahim's wife went out to the terraced plot to throw two handfuls of corn to the hungry chickens, she saw her husband entering the yard in his old robe and heading for the sunshade and then arranging its torn bags spread on the neglected branches. The woman rubbed her eyes thinking she was seeing a false vision. But no. This was Ibrahim, the one and only. Her heart beat violently, and she ran toward him shouting, "Ibrahim!"

He gave her a quick look then returned to his things heaped

on the ground, bending over them and looking for something. He said, "Where is my ax, Wife? Where is the hammer? Where is the chisel?"

She asked in surprise, "What do you intend to do with them?"

He said, "I left them here. Who took them away from their place?"

She said, "Here they are. Sorry, the chickens left their droppings on them. . . ."

He said, "That's all right. I'll clean and wash them." He then looked around and said, "We still have several good-sized rocks, thank God. Quick, Wife, fry me two eggs for breakfast. I will prepare the tools. People are in need of millstones after I have left my work all this time. . . ."

A few days later, the hermit descended to the village and thought of passing by the hut of Ibrahim's wife to see how she was doing. And lo, he saw Ibrahim sitting cross-legged under his sunshade chiseling a stone. As soon as the millstone maker noticed him, he stood up, rushed to him, and warmly embraced him while tears were flowing from his eyes. Malik's eyes welled up with tears, too, and he kissed him on the cheeks.

Ibrahim shouted, "Wife, come and greet our beloved hermit. . . . And fry him two eggs. . . ."

The hermit said, "No, no. A bowl of water is enough for me."

Ibrahim took him by the hand and sat him on a rock beside him, and he himself sat down among the stone chips. Malik said, "Your absence has been long, Ibrahim."

"Indeed," said Ibrahim. "My absence has been long. But here I am, finally. . . . I've come back."

The hermit took the bowl of water from Ibrahim's wife and said as he was raising it to his lips, "You've then returned to the making of millstones, have you?"

"Yes," he answered. "I've returned to the making of millstones, Malik. And I've also returned to the fear and love of God."

The hermit drank the water in one gulp, some of it spilling

on his mustache and long, unkempt beard, and he said, "How delicious your water is this morning! I shall not need to drink again all day today."

He then stood up, bade them farewell, and left.

. . .

This is one of many stories my father used to tell again and again in the evenings after he came home from work and after we had supper together and whetted our minds to listen to his words. If he was not too tired, he prolonged the narration, padded the dialogue, and elaborated on the description. Many of those stories, which if not originally from *The Thousand and One Nights,* were derived from it as I discovered when I grew up, had themes that glorified virtue, ascetic life, and poverty.

Most probably, Malik the hermit was one of the models or heroes that my father unconsciously adopted. Perhaps another model hero was Ibrahim the millstone maker before he was corrupted by wealth. My father was convinced that it was easier for a camel to pass through the eye of a needle than for a rich man to enter Paradise. It was important for my father to enter Paradise in order to see the face of his Lord. He never asked for anything in the world other than for the least that life could give to sustain him and his family. In that, he thought, there was wealth and sufficiency for him.

 12

In the fall of 1928, my brother Yusuf rebelled against the Syriac School. He made up his mind that he was not learning anything new in it. He was twelve years old or a little older. So he began to read books that he happened upon or magazines sold in the market, of which he read as many articles as he could in collusion with the seller, before the few copies were sold out. My eldest brother, Murad, had left St. Mark's Monastery in Jerusalem and begun to learn carpentry. Yusuf felt, after his visits to

Murad's workshop, that there was more for him to learn in it than at the miserable little school crowded with boys.

However, before falling prey to the lure of carpentry, he decided to enter the government school. He learned from some of his friends that teaching there was free, that each subject was taught by a specialized teacher, and that graduates could become government employees at a monthly salary amounting possibly to three and perhaps four pounds. Without telling anyone at home, Yusuf went one morning to the National School of Bethlehem, and its principal welcomed him immediately and admitted him to the third elementary class.

That was a tremendous change, not only for him, but also for me because he came home every day and showed me his books and copybooks and told me what this or that teacher said, thus arousing in me a strange yearning for his new world.

One evening, he sat me next to him and opened his English book to read me the story of "Aladdin and the Lamp." We were sitting on the mat, thumbing through the pages of the *New Method Readers* book in the light of the kerosene lamp, our imagination flying from our dim lamp to Aladdin's magic lamp which, as soon as he rubbed it, made a genie appear who realized miracles for him.

I said, "I want to enter the National School like you." By doing that, I felt as though I would obtain Aladdin's lamp.

He said, "They will not accept you now because the first term has almost ended. You have to wait until the beginning of the coming school year."

And I waited.

At the end of the first term, Yusuf came running home and announced that he was first in his class. . . . A month or two after that, Teacher Jabboor told him that he was wrongly placed in the third class and that, starting from the third term, he would be promoted to the fourth class so that he would enter the fifth class at the beginning of the following school year. Being first in his class, he wished he could be promoted to a higher class every month, for he felt he was the most clever of all the students around him.

Yusuf's hair was long and thick, and he boasted of it among his friends. When the principal one morning announced to the students standing in line on the playground that new instructions from the Department of Education required all students to have their hair cut by clippers at zero degrees or at one degree of length at most, Yusuf felt that the matter concerned the other boys, and absolutely not him at all.

Though reluctantly, the boys began to have their hair cut —but not Yusuf. The principal began to take strict measures to implement the directive, which had been circulated to all government schools in Palestine in those days and to which students did not respond warmly. The principal then threatened to kick any student out of school who did not have his hair cut. Yusuf persisted in his obstinacy until the principal said to him one day, "If you come to me tomorrow with this long hair of yours, I shall send you back home. Do you understand?"

On the following day, Yusuf went to school, having combed his long hair as he did every day. When the principal saw him in the playground, now very strange looking with his thick hair hanging behind his ears among the hundreds of boys with clean-shorn heads, he immediately called him and shook his cane at him. However, being fond of him because he was first in his class and because his teachers praised him for his intelligence, the principal said to him, "Yusuf, go immediately to the barber and don't return until he has finished cutting these locks off your head. Do you hear me? I'll be waiting for you. Go quickly!"

Yusuf left at once, carrying his bag of books—and he did not return to school. He refused to have his hair cut because he felt that he did not need the school in the first place; that he could teach himself by himself, or so he imagined; and that he had, in any case, to look for a job and earn some money after my father had begun to show signs of illness. Yusuf realized that the money my father brought home at the end of the week was not sufficient for our daily needs. The issue of having his hair cut was secondary for him. No, he would never be seen with a clean-shorn head. Let the principal do what he would with the instructions and orders he wanted to apply to boys' heads.

He went to a grocery whose owner was a well-known Armenian named Khugaz. It was at the bottom of the steps leading to the Municipal Market. Khugaz was a middle-aged, short, and fat man who had inwardly begun to feel the weakness of oncoming old age. He had known Murad and Yusuf for some time and had often asked them to work for him at the shop, helping him to sell candies, pickles, rice, and lentils. In fact, Murad had worked for him for several months before he began to work at the carpentry shop of Abu Akila.

Khugaz hardly believed his eyes when he saw Yusuf standing before him saying, "I've come to work for you."

Khugaz asked him, "What about school, my son?"

He answered, "I was to be promoted to the fourth class, then to the fifth, but I would not have my hair cut. What do you want me to do?"

"Come, enter. First, observe me attentively as I deal with people and note how I treat customers. Do like me. They say you are good at arithmetic. Remember what you sell and record it in this book as soon as it is sold. Come on, pull yourself together now and show me how determined you are to work well."

That was the last my brother Yusuf saw of school.

However, if school was too narrow to contain his ambition, Khugaz's shop was not alluring enough to keep him for long, though he came to know many people of the neighborhood through it. He soon moved on to another job, then to another. In two or three years, he had tried several different occupations and finally settled on carpentry. He carried a saw in one hand and books and magazines in the other. His wages were always minuscule and hardly sufficient to provide the family with bare existence when added to my father's income.

■　■　■

What a significant morning it was in my life when I wore my only good jacket and unpatched shorts and my polished shoes, and went out to Ras Iftays Street, full of apprehension and delightful expectation. I hurried to Nativity Square and from it to the alleys behind the Church of the Nativity leading to the National School. That was on the opening day of schools toward the end of September 1929.

On the way, near the mosque and just by the confectioner of *ma'mool* pastries, I met a boy who knew me. He was unpleasant to me and wanted me to accompany him to play in the market. But I left with firm determination saying, "I want to go the National School." I dodged him and ran, feeling terribly annoyed by the shoes I wore, but I had to bear them and get accustomed to them for the sake of my new school—if I was admitted to it.

The wide iron gate appealed to me. Above it was a large sign written in beautiful calligraphy which said "The National School of Bethlehem." I was instantly filled with a strange pride and felt that the school belonged to me and I to it. I entered the front yard apprehensively and saw some boys playing, of whom I recognized no one. I headed for the school building, whose doors and windows had been recently painted green, and I saw teachers going to and fro. After some hesitation, I summoned up my courage and asked someone, "Where is Teacher Jabboor, please?"

He was my brother's favorite teacher, and my brother had advised me to ask for him, shake hands with him, and tell him who I was.

A tall teacher in an elegant suit came, walking slowly in the portico with a book in his hand. "This is Teacher Jabboor," I was told.

I approached him shyly and said, my tongue almost tied and my heart beating strongly against my ribs, "I am Yusuf Ibrahim's brother."

I was surprised at his warm answer, "Oh where is that smart naughty boy? Why has he not returned to school?"

I said, "He works now. And he sent me to you so that you may help me gain admission to school."

He gave me a long look with his blue eyes and lit a cigarette. Then he said, "Come."

He led me to a room on whose door was written "The

Principal." The man was skinny with white hair, and he wore metal-rimmed glasses. He was standing and talking to one of the students. The sun filled his little room, and this, for some reason, mitigated my fear of meeting that principal about whom my brother had often spoken as though he were a legendary person.

Teacher Jabboor said, "Mr. Fadeel, this boy is the brother of Yusuf Ibrahim. Do you remember Yusuf? He was the first in his class, and you intended to promote him to a higher class, one or two grades ahead."

Mr. Fadeel dismissed the student who was with him and answered in a high-pitched voice and in a dialect which was not Bethlehemite (I knew he was from Nazareth and Teacher Jabboor was from Umm al-Fahm, one of the villages near Nazareth): "I remember him; I remember him . . . what has become of that boy?"

The teacher answered, "He works now in order to help his family, no doubt. I hope you will agree to admit his brother to our school."

He scrutinized me. I had not said anything yet. He then picked up a book from his desk, opened it at random, and thrust it toward me, still open, saying, "Read, from the top of the page."

With dry lips, I read three or four lines while the principal and the teacher listened and nodded. Then Mr. Fadeel said, "Enough, enough."

He addressed the teacher, "Like his brother?"

The teacher smiled, "Most probably."

"Third class?"

"That's reasonable."

The principal suddenly turned around and sat at his desk. He took out a copybook from the drawer, turned a few pages, then took a fountain pen from an inner pocket and asked, "What's your name?"

I said, "Jabra Ibrahim."

"Fine. How old are you?"

"Nine years."

He recorded that in his copybook, stood up, and said, "Please, go to your class . . . the third class."

I was about to jump for joy at the door when he stopped me at the threshold saying in a loud voice, "Listen! Your hair is still long . . . come tomorrow, after having it cut with the clippers. Do you hear me?"

Teacher Jabboor accompanied me in the sunny portico running along the edge of a little garden with pine trees. We then turned into another portico with a succession of classrooms, at the end of which was a door with a little piece of wood on its border, on which was written "The Third Class." He made me enter a large room full of boys of all ages. In it was a young teacher carrying an English book, in fact the same book from which Yusuf had read to me the story of "Aladdin and the Lamp."

"Mr. Faheem, this is a new student. Do you have a place for him?"

"Yes. He will sit there, near Shihada."

In all the schools I had been to until then, the only student seats I knew were the long ones which five or more boys could sit on. Here, however, each of the seats seated two boys only, and some of them were empty. I sat down in the place designated for me by Teacher Faheem, almost dizzy with excitement, apprehension, and joy. Teacher Jabboor went out, reassured that he had left me in trustworthy hands. Shihada placed his open book in front of me so that I could share it with him, but I understood nothing of what the teacher was saying. When the bell rang and the boys were about to leave, the teacher signaled to me to remain behind until they had all left.

He asked me, "Do you have any books?"

I said, "No."

He said, "Well then, come with me."

I walked with him to a room on whose door was written "The Storeroom." He asked a man sitting there at a table, on which were piles of books and papers, to give me the books of the third class. After a while, the bell rang again and the students returned to their classes, and I went back to sit next to

Shihada. I now had two or three Arabic and English books, a copybook for drawing and another for calligraphy, and I felt they were the keys to the doors of Paradise. I had only to hurry to them, open them, and see amazing things that had never occurred to me.

■ ■ ■

Every morning, noon, and evening, I crossed Nativity Square on my way between my home and school. It was the permanent meeting place of schoolboys and schoolgirls, as well as travelers, worshipers, visitors, monks, nuns, and tourists of all kinds; it was the meeting place of fashions, forms, and sounds. In the part next to the Municipality Building which was shaded by a giant pine tree, there were restaurants and cafés that were never without clients, the most famous being Abu Zaki's restaurant, which was characterized by the fact that its fat and cheerful owner Abu Zaki was always busy making *hummus mudammas* (chickpea dip with sesame cream, lemon, garlic, and spices) by pounding it at the wide-open door of the restaurant. He had put a large poster on the wall, showing the face of a young man with long sideburns reaching his jaws, and with full lips and dreamy eyes. On the top, large writing said "The singer of kings and princes, Muhammad Abdul-Wahhab." Opposite it was a similar large poster showing a woman with long braids and a tight black headkerchief from which a lock of hair curled on her forehead. On the poster was written "The star of the East, Umm Kulthum." On a little table near the door was a gramophone with a big horn directed toward the street, from which a song was continuously blaring. Entitled "Ya Jaratal-Wadi" ("O Neighbor of the Valley"), the song was soon learned by my friends and me, and we vied with one another for the longest breath while singing its first words.

In the first few days, the school atmosphere made me feel isolated and anguished. But this feeling did not last long, especially after I befriended two or three boys, for we banded together in the playground as a group resisting the older boys. Like all the other classes, the third class did not consist of a homogeneous group: it contained a variety of forms, ages, clothing, and dialects. Some of the boys in my class were my age; others were older and could have been fourteen years old or even older. Some were tall and had deep manly voices. Among them were some who wore gowns; others wore shorts or trousers. Some wore shoes and socks; some wore shoes without socks; and others were barefoot and had dusty feet and soiled legs. There were those who wore fezzes, caps, headkerchiefs with a black rope, or casquettes. We realized that having our hair cut with clippers, at zero degrees sometimes, was a health measure to protect against lice, which infested the heads of those with long hair. As soon as we entered the classroom, we had to take off our head gear, and we sometimes saw boys who kept their eyes on the fleas that jumped off their heads onto the desks in the direction of their classmates. When Teacher Jabboor mentioned one day that there was a solecism which Arab grammarians called the language of "the fleas, they ate me," the image was very clear in my mind: there was a period of my life in which I experienced fleas that "ate" me mercilessly every night, and I was at a loss what to do about them, especially when we lived in *al-khashashi* (the huts).

The boys at school spoke varying dialects, though all were understood by everyone. There were the distinctive dialects of Bethlehem, Bayt Sahoor, Bayt Jala, Hebron, Bayt Faghoor, and Bani Taamar. Furthermore, some boys were Christians and some Muslims; and the Christians, who were the majority, included some who were Greek Orthodox and others who were Latins, Syriacs, Catholics, or Armenians. From this big human mixture, Mr. Fadeel Nimr and the teaching staff he headed (Jabboor Abbood, Faheem Jabboor, Elias Hamati, Husam Ishtayya, and others) tried hard, as he repeated on several occasions, to create a harmonious school, which would plant good manners and high ideals in the hearts of students as well as the love of knowledge and learning, so that they might all put these in the service of the idea of Arabism, and especially the Arabism of Palestine.

The teachers took pride in their students when an inspector

from the Department of Education came. Inspectors visited frequently in those days, and the names of some of them are unforgettable: like Khalil al-Sakakini and, later, Isaaf al-Nashashibi and Shaykh Husam Jar-Allah.

The inspector who impressed us most was Khalil al-Sakakini with his ever freshly ironed red fez perfectly placed on his thick black hair beginning to turn gray, his elegant jacket in the buttonhole of which he always had a rose while visiting us, and his clear classical Arabic which he spoke with a resonant voice despite its strange huskiness, pronouncing his words melodiously and making them not only enchanting to hear but also easy to understand.

As for Isaaf al-Nashashibi, he was very short and wore high-heeled shoes. In spite of his noticeably elegant appearance, he did not impress one on first sight until he began to speak: he spoke in an amazing rhythmic language that bewitched us with its rhymes, but we understood only a few of its words; and yet, when he left us, we abided in an ecstasy we did not comprehend.

From time to time, an English inspector came to our classroom. His appearance was awe inspiring, and his thick eyebrows above his glasses looked like two little bushes planted in his forehead. His name was Mr. Farrell. One day, he surprised Teacher Faheem, who was giving us an English lesson. Mr. Farrell asked us about the meaning of certain words and the spelling of a few simple ones, and so we gave him correct answers. Then he said, "And now, who can write the word 'beautiful' on the board?"

The teacher was a little disturbed and said it was a long and difficult word.

He looked around at the boys with some hope and much despair. Alone among them, I had raised my hand. Mr. Farrell was not convinced of my courage, so he said to me in a heavily accented Arabic, "Come and write it on the board."

I went up to the blackboard full of anxiety and apprehension. He gave me a piece of chalk and I wrote "beautiful." Teacher Faheem exclaimed, "Wonderful!" Mr. Farrell was astonished, and his deep eyes shone behind his glasses and under his thick eyebrows, and he said, "Very good! What is the name of this boy?" He recorded some remark in his notebook. Most probably, what he recorded at that moment made him remember my name many years later and have an influence on my studies, although I was unaware of that.

Teacher Faheem laughed joyfully and said, "You have stood me in good stead, God bless you!"*

My going to the National School at the age of nine was the beginning of my real exposure to life. As though by a touch of Aladdin's lamp, I experienced an opening up to people of all kinds from whom I had been isolated by my family inside a little cocoon on the margin of everything. I had to try my muscles with weights of which I had no knowledge. Teeming with dreamy visions nourished on church tunes and on wanderings among trees, rocks, valleys, mountains, and distant horizons, my mind now had also to contend with the experience of interacting with hundreds of students of different ages and inclinations, and every hour that I listened to my teachers' words brought something new to me.

In the poetry anthology prepared by Isaaf al-Nashashibi for schools, entitled *Al-Bustan* (*The Garden*) and distributed to us without charge, there was a beautiful strange world for me, a past which gradually began to take shape and be embodied in my imagination through the short poems whose verses the anthologist had expertly selected and explained. Whether I understood them or not, I began learning many of those poems by heart, and I declaimed them aloud, as though I were addressing the olive trees and the vines, whenever I climbed up a tree or stood on a terrace wall on the edge of the valley. The language itself moved me with its words and rhythms, how much more it would have if I had understood more of their meanings! Jabboor Abbood, the teacher of Arabic, chose heroic

*When I saw Teacher Faheem in Bethlehem about twenty years later in 1948, after I had returned from England and had worked as a professor of English literature at the Rashidiyya College in Jerusalem, the first thing he reminded me of was that little incident which, I don't know why, he never forgot, nor did I.

poems from this anthology and required us to learn them by heart as class assignments. How wonderful it was for the throat to say aloud:

> I am from the people who remain unimpaired.
> When a noble chieftain dies, another rises instead.

How immensely I enjoyed pronouncing the name of the poet Amr ibn Maadikarib! I have continued to love him since the day I imagined him as an old man about a hundred years old yet still a "young man" full of vitality and pride, jumping onto his horse's back in a flash, saying:

> When I saw our women scurrying on the stony ground
> And Lameece among them like the full moon in the sky. . . .

He rushed on horseback to the battlefield to fight and become immersed in the battle, his sword rising and falling, as his people were being stricken down. As for him, he conquered death and time:

> I am not worried or afraid, tears avail me nothing.
> Those I love are gone and like the sword I abide alone.

I imagined myself like the poet fighting in battlefields in which swords and spears clashed until, like him, I remained alone like the sword.

This identification with the poets became an unconscious custom of mine. It doubled the joy of what I read and made me always look for more. I was particularly charmed by poets who boasted of their courage and loneliness; and in my adolescence, a few years later, this gave special magic to the effect that Malik ibn al-Rayb's famous poem had on my soul:

> Don't you see that I've sold error for guidance
> And joined Ibn Affan's invading army?

I repeated some of his verses in which he elegized himself:

> I recalled those who lamented me but found none
> But my sword and my Rudayni spear

And my reddish horse dragging its bridle to the water,
Fate having bereft it of the one who took it to drink.

I imagined his horse, its rider having fallen to the ground, stained with blood, one of his feet perhaps still caught in the stirrup; and I visualized the horse, dragging the dead poet to the water. In my continuing daydream, I put myself in his shoes and went on saying:

But on the edges of the arena, there are women
Who take my predicament dearly to heart.

And at that tragic moment, I asked of my two companions what Malik had asked when he realized that his adventures were coming to an end:

Dig my grave with spearheads
And cover my eyes with the edge of my garment.
And don't begrudge me a large plot, God bless you,
The earth is wide enough.
Take me, drag my body to you in my cloak.
In previous days, I was hard to control.

That fateful event was to come later on in the poet's life. But in 1929 and in the year following it, the anti-Zionist revolt had spread again all over the country, and we began to learn nationalistic songs, and we repeated:

We are God's soldiers, the youth of the land.
We abhor humiliation and reject oppression.

We sang aloud with tireless voices and in more than one tune:

Darkness of prison, reign. We fear not the dark.
After night, only glory dawns and rises high.

Like words etched in polished steel, words and their meanings raged in our souls and our young minds like stormy winds.

Fadeel Nimr, the principal, was a poet who loved music and played it. We sometimes saw him coming to school in the morning, carrying a violin in its long, black box. This made him appear less terrifying to the students than when he was inspecting the classes with a stick in his hand. After he heard my voice and found it strong and high, he chose me to be a member of the school choir, which he taught to sing stirring fiery songs as well as "welcoming" songs, some of which were his own compositions, and he accompanied us on his violin. He organized more than one ceremony, and he trained us to welcome the guests by songs with words like these:

Welcome, distinguished and eminent people.
Your geniality has clearly shone in this place.

Then we changed the tune and sang again, while he led the choir, played the violin, and kept the time by tapping the floor with the toe of his left foot with some force lest we lose the rhythm. When finally the audience applauded, he laid the violin and bow aside, took out a piece of paper from his pocket, and read from it a laudatory address using grand figures of speech that compensated for the versified inane words of welcome forced upon him by the occasion.

Teacher Elias Hamati taught us arithmetic and made us look forward to the promised day when he would teach us algebra and geometry. Teacher Abbas taught us ancient history and prepared us to study Arab history in the following year. Teacher Faheem who, it became clear, had just graduated from Teachers' Training College (the Arab College) in Jerusalem, taught us English as well as physical education. He amazed us with his strong, athletic body and the difficult exercises he gave us to do; he was almost always angry with us for not being able to balance as well as he or exercise in unison. But when he smiled, we were elated, even if only for a few moments.

The only other teacher who equaled him in anger when irritated was the calligraphy teacher, Husam Ishtayya. He was extremely gentle, mild, and convincing; and his speech, which was tinged with the dialect of Cairo where he had studied calligraphy, sounded to us like singing. But when he erupted like a volcano at the misbehavior or bad penmanship of certain students, he did not hesitate to use the broad ruler to forcefully strike their palms and make us all feel the tension in the air. What this artist calligrapher taught me in that year about Arabic calligraphy opened my eyes to the delicate world of visual forms and put me in touch with a sensibility for the written word, on both counts enriching my aesthetic experience for all the days of my life.

What also helped me in this regard was that Shihada Abdul-Samee, who was my schoolmate, was a calligrapher despite his young age. He was very dark and was perhaps two or three years older than I was. Before his family decided to settle in Bethlehem, he had spent some time working in Jerusalem with a calligrapher, who wrote commercial signs. Shihada's father was from Hebron and wove mats and made jute bags; his little shop was on Nativity Square opposite the Municipality Building. Besides housing City Hall, this building also contained the police station and a lockup from whose windows arrested prisoners looked out on passersby and asked them to throw them "a cigarette for God's sake." It also had a clinic popularly called "the health center," whose main concerns were inoculation for diseases, vaccinating children against smallpox, fighting malaria by treating the water of cisterns with petroleum from time to time in order to kill the mosquitoes breeding in them, and controlling stray dogs by collecting them in cages and giving them poisoned meat. One of the common disparaging remarks one of us would say in jest to another was, "It is better for you that the health center take charge of you." Shihada and I often went to his father's shop on being dismissed from school. We sat on a mat among the piles of rolled up mats, and he showed me the Qur'anic verses he wrote in an astonishingly masterly way for a person of his age. He taught me how to cut a reed, make a pen of it, and write like him. While Teacher Husam concentrated on teaching us the rules of the cursive calligraphy called Ruqaa, Shihada taught me the calligraphy rules of Thuluth, Farisi, and what he called Humayooni.

Shihada was afflicted with ophthalmia, and the dust of the mats and jute bags was not merciful to his eyes; and so he had to leave school at the end of that academic year. This saddened me greatly despite the fact that our friendship continued until he returned to Hebron a few months later.

More important than all that was the Arabic language I was taught by Teacher Jabboor Abbood. He infected us with his love for the language, and his lesson was not limited to the official syllabus of that year. Of the grammatical rules of the language, he taught me in two years, or a little over, more than I ever learned from anybody else, and what he taught me has remained basic in my dealings with writing up to the present. He was fond of parsing difficult poetic verses, and like him, I began to find pleasure in following the complex relationships between words, for these are logical and rational relationships similar to mathematical relationships between parts of algebraic equations. When he said to me, "Parse the following: 'O driver of camels, crossing the deserts, / Kindly halt at the sand dunes of Tayy,'" I found great pleasure in parsing the verse. He then said, "That was an easy verse. Parse now this one for me, if you are really clever." He dictated a verse full of morphological and syntactical puzzles, and I tried to respond to his challenge, analyzing the words one by one and hoping to come to grips with their cryptic nature and their syntax, sometimes with his help and sometimes without, until I extricated myself somehow from my difficulty.

■ ■ ■

I did not believe what I heard the teacher say in the presence of all the class: I was the first!

I never competed with anyone, and I kept away from competing with others during all the years of my education. In fact, the spirit of competition was alien to my thought and my way of life. However, the important thing was that I, who felt in earlier days that I had been forcibly plunged into a group of strangers, was now the first among them. The term reports distributed to us testified to this fact. Perhaps it was not important for the school that I know this result. The important thing was that the other students know it in order to kindle in them the spirit of competition.

There was at least one student, older and taller than I was, who wore a gown reaching to his heels and a high fez of a wonderful red color, both emphasizing his height. His name was Elias. I saw him objecting and crying, and raising his voice in the portico in anger because he expected to be the first. He had come from Bayt Sahoor, loaded with special recommendations to all the teachers. He had not joined the school late like me, and lo, he was only the second.

I did not give the matter much attention. Elias began to play less with us on the playground because he became preoccupied with studying—or what we used to call cramming. The result at the end of the year was what he had wanted. I remained the one with the highest marks in Arabic, English, and history—yet he was the first, and I the second. In the following year, he lost his favored position in a strange manner when it was acquired by a new classmate of ours who came from the Greek Orthodox School. His name was Yaqoub. He became the first, and I the second. As for Elias, his position fell back to the fifth or the sixth.

I was several times in later years ranked lower in my classes than students who were truly intelligent and outstanding and who had a clear influence on Arab life after they graduated from university. The spirit of student competition in class motivated them strongly, while I cared for nothing but following my lessons and readings, in my own way and according to my own natural disposition, not competing with anyone and not heeding the competition of anyone.

Perhaps the reason was that I had begun to say, even at that early time, that I might drop out of school at any moment as my brother before me. However much I enjoyed its lessons, school was not for me because my father's sickness began to worsen and to frighten us all. It was said his problem was sciatica. Since his job at the hospital of the Sisters of Charity was very strenuous, the pain in his left leg came as a frightful warning to him and the family. He was the hospital gardener, but he was also much more than that. Whenever there was a heavy bag that had to be carried from the gate, up the stairs, and through a long corridor to the kitchen, he was the one to carry it. And whenever there was a large piece of furniture to be moved from one room to another, he was the one to move it. And whenever there was a terrace or a field to be plowed, he was the one to plow it. He started working at sunrise and came back home only in the early dusk. He boasted that Ma Soeur Janine, the chief supervisor among the nuns (who were all French), was proud of him and did not do anything in the hospital, outside the patients' rooms, unless he was at her side. She spoke to him in an Arabicized French or in a Frenchified Arabic, which he found to be cute coming from her and which he imitated at home for our entertainment. When he was absent for a day, she sent someone to our home to ask about him. Yet in spite of all this, I began to be aware that his daily effort was not commensurate with the few piasters he earned as a daily wage for all that work. What Yusuf had done was inevitable, and now was my turn: we must both work and permit my father to rest from his hard work.

However, when I told my brother, at the beginning of the summer holidays, that I wanted to leave school in order to share with him the family's responsibilities, he yelled at me, giving me one of those shouts he was famous for. He seized me by the collar of my shirt and shook me fiercely, saying, "By God, if I ever hear you say such a thing again, I will hit you so hard that the angels will hear your screams! What can a child like you do for a job? Do you want to carry a basket on your back in the market and be a porter of people's things? You will stay at school, as long as there is a school!"

In turn, I shouted back, "And you, why did you leave school? Were you not the first in your class?"

He said, "Is it necessary that my misfortune be also yours? Furthermore, I am . . . older . . . I am fully fourteen years old, and going on fifteen . . . I am able to work and study at the same time. Don't you see all these books of mine? As for you. . . ."

Becoming aware that we were arguing, my mother asked Yusuf, "Why are you shouting at your brother?"

"Because this mister wants to drop out of school. He wants to help us earn our livelihood."

My mother laughed, "Something must have affected his brains!"

I said, "Well, I'm crazy. Permit me to be crazy."

She said, "First, you have to grow up, Son. Then, God will dispose. Our Lord will always provide us with our livelihood. Your school is more important now."

When my father heard the summary of this conversation that evening, he said, "By God, so long as I have pulse in my veins and breath in my chest, I shall never allow you to drop out of school. Your brother did what he did last year only in disobedience to me. If it were up to me, I would return him to school tomorrow—and let us die of hunger. Do you both want to be illiterate like me when you become adults?"

(And I remembered what my father had related more than once about the few days he had spent at school in his childhood. He had learned all the alphabet, he said, but after two or three weeks he had to take the sheep out to pasture with his father and to help him plow the fields by driving two huge yoked oxen back and forth in straight furrows from sunrise to sunset. What he had learned fast, he also forgot fast.)

My father added, "I rejoice immensely, and so does this mother of yours, when we see you both reading books. Why? Because the word is holy. Yes, indeed. The word is from God. Rather, the Word is God, as the Gospel says. The word is the book. Or am I mistaken?"

 13

In that year, my father was blessed, or rather we were all blessed, with the birth of a baby girl he named Susan after his mother who had died during the First World War. She was the eighth child of my mother, who had earlier given birth to seven boys; one was stillborn and two had died in childhood. Susan was the beloved of everyone; she was pampered by the adults and the children, and we nicknamed her Shusha.

With her birth, the family decided that the Fathu house was no longer large enough for us and that we had to look for another one. We did not go far this time, for my father learned that there was a house at the top of the road which we took back home daily; it consisted of a large room with a broken door and rickety windows, all of which my father and brothers took upon themselves to repair. Next to it was a hut (miserable, of course, but useful) and a vast courtyard, in the middle of which was a deep well and in front of which was a large terraced plot with trees. The whole place looked out on to the road and was separate from any other building. Because of its elevated position, it overlooked the new road to Jerusalem, the Jamal valley, the hills behind it, the blue mountains beyond, and the whole world! On the other side of the road, there was a large terraced plot belonging to the house, but it was without trees. We did not hesitate at all: in only two days we moved, sheep, chickens, and all, to Jahluqa's house.

At first, the proprietor's name frightened me, and I imagined him with wide-open bulging eyes, as his name suggested, and with a poxed face and canine teeth protruding between his thick lips. I saw only his old wife, who was no different from any other old woman, when she came to my mother to collect the balance of the rent, having earlier received a down payment on the yearly rent of four pounds. As for Jahluqa himself, I imagined that he never left his home at Duhaysha lest people see his ugliness. I was greatly disappointed when he later visited us, and I found he was a poor old man with a kind face and gentle speech, whose walking stick never left him, even when he sat on the floor, for then he put it between his knees to lean on again when getting up.

I thought that Bethlehemites—like other human beings, as I later discovered—did not have mercy on one another with the nicknames they exchanged. Such nicknames stuck to them whether they liked them or not. And in spite of the fact that they initially resisted them and rebelled at the injustice of them, they were mostly obliged to accept them submissively, because everyone else insisted on the names and called them by no others. But

woe betide anyone with a disability, for it became his nickname
and that of his family, and it continued to live for generations
after him! There were families with names like al-Aʿmā (the
Blind), al-Aʿraj (the Lame), al-ʿArrāj (the Hobbler), Quṭaysh
(Shorty), al-Akhras (the Dumb), al-Aṭrash (the Deaf), al-Aḥdab
(the Hunchback), Jaḥlūqa (Goggle-Eyed), and Qurrāʿa (Bald-
headed). An incident might happen to someone involving an
insect or an animal, and he would acquire a new name that stuck;
as a result, there were families named Ṣarṣūr (Cockroach) rendered milder as Ṣanṣūr, Dhubbāna (Fly), Dabdūb (Bear Tread),
Ḥazbūn (Cock), al-Fār (the Mouse), al-Jamal (the Camel), al-
Baghla (the Mule), al-Ḥīḥī (the Donkey), and al-Jaʿʿār (the
Brayer). He whose name came to him on account of a bird might
be more fortunate, and similarly so if it came on account of a
vegetable, plant, or fruit, for there were nicknames like Ḥamāma
(Pigeon), Ṣūṣ (Chick), Dīk (Rooster), and Zarzar (Singing Bird)
or Faqqūsa (Cucumber), Fulayfil (Pepper), Ḥanẓal (Colocynth),
Rummāna (Pomegranate), Tuffāḥa (Apple), Daḥbūra (Water-
melon), and Maḥshī (Stuffed Marrow). Happiest of all was
someone whose grandfather or grandmother was of such power
and influence to retain his mere name for all the grandchildren
and great-grandchildren. However, names of professions were
still common like Ḥaddād (Smith), Najjār (Carpenter), Naqqār
(Chiseler), Ḥajjār (Stone Cutter), Qaṭṭān (Cotton Dealer),
Farrān (Baker), Qanawātī (Canal Digger), and Saḥḥār (Magician).
Nicknames like Farḥān (Joyful Man), Farḥā (Joyful Woman),
Ḥazīn (Sorrowful Man), and Ḥazīna (Sorrowful Woman) went
back, like all others, to ages so distant in the past that no one
remembered any longer where and when they originated, and
who was the first Joyful Man or Sorrowful Woman.

All this did not prevent the people, Arab and non-Arab,
from repeating, without much knowledge of history, that
they descended originally from two big tribes named Qays
and Yaman, several clans of which had settled in the area of
Bethlehem—including the villages surrounding it such as Bayt
Jala, Bayt Sahoor, Irtas, al-Khadir, and Batteer. Thus there were
families which somehow traced their lineage back to the Qays

and others to the Yaman. That was a spontaneous confirmation of the Arab origin of a town built by the Canaanites at the beginning of the second millennium B.C. and named the "House of Bread," which is the meaning of the ancient Aramaic name of Bethlehem, where the wheat, barley, and millet crops from the fertile fields stretching for miles around the town were gathered, constituting the staple food of the people in it and in nearby Jerusalem. This explains why in ancient times it was a center for the worship of Tammuz, the god of fertility. In addition, there were those who believed that, in the early centuries of the Christian era, the Byzantines left their influence by intermarrying with the original inhabitants, as the Crusaders did later on. All of these influences have been integrated into the great Arab stream.

■   ■   ■

With what renewed determination my father plowed the large terraced plot on the other side of the road! Having been deprived of his land for about twenty years, now he had a plot—though rented—which he could plow for himself and his children. We helped him as much as we could, listening to the stories he told about the hardships of his childhood and boyhood. We sowed the land with barley and said the crop would be a new means of subsistence for us.

In the other terraced plot with trees, parallel to the court-yard and the well in front of the house, I found that I could do something which would not prevent me from continuing my schooling and which would help the family at the same time. My father brought me seedlings of cauliflower and cabbage, and he entrusted me with planting them. I mentally drew lines on the ground, then I dug small holes at regular distances and planted the seedlings one by one. The water was nearby. We did not need to buy it this time or to carry it in cans from the wells of others, for our well was large and full, and it had a mouth stone that had become polished and grooved with deep, smooth notches by the bucket ropes used over the years. I drew water in the bucket, collected it in a can, took the can to the terraced plot, and watered the seedlings in carefully measured amounts. Whenever I got tired, the big mulberry tree on the edge of the plot was my secure refuge. I climbed it with my school books. Among its branches and leaves, I could raise my voice to read. I could also raise it to sing, and I felt that my singing gushed into the valley, filled it, and overflowed the mountain tops. My friend, Anton Du‘ayk, might look out at me from the balcony of a high house, one hundred meters away from ours. His large house with its three stories had many rooms and several balconies. He might call out to me from the balcony, and I would answer him shouting, "Come to my tree and study with me!" In the morning, we met on the street and went to school together. He might ask me to explain to him this or that lesson before we sat in our seats in class.

In that year, we were obliged to adopt new means of livelihood because my father found himself unable to continue working at the nuns' hospital. Our chickens multiplied by continuous hatching. My mother one day initiated a strange plan: one of the chickens was in a "clucking" mood, and so my mother bought ten duck eggs and made the deceived chicken sit on them. We waited anxiously for the result. Would the eggs hatch really? And if they did, would the chicks live? Or would the chicken discover its mistake and reject them?

The clucking chicken remained on the eggs for twenty-one days, which we counted together in expectation of the happy day. Early in the morning of the last day, I hurried to the coop in the hut, and I shouted joyfully when I saw nine ducklings peeping around the hen. The tenth egg was spoilt.

The ducklings grew and ran behind their "mother" among the chickens. When it rained, I dug a small depression for them in which the water quickly gathered, and the ducklings jumped into it to swim while the mother hen stood at the edge, perplexed by this odd behavior and trying not to fall into the water! Perhaps she then realized that she had been deceived and exploited. Nonetheless, in a few months, we had nine big ducks which, when they began to lay eggs, gave us the opportunity to start hatching more of them and selling them.

However, pigs were the greatest addition that year. Raising three or four sheep did not bring us much profit when we sold them. Real profit—my father was told—lay in pigs. You only had to buy a few piglets at a low price and raise them; in a year or less, they grew and became fat, after the males were neutered, and each of them weighed as much as seventy or eighty kilograms or more.

In the meantime, my brother Yusuf had been obliged to go to Jerusalem to work because his employer at the carpentry shop refused to raise his meager wage. He took with him my beloved grandmother to take care of his affairs in the little room he rented in the Old City of Jerusalem. My brother Murad had preceded him to Jerusalem some time earlier in order to enjoy his independence, as was his custom, and all the opportunities for finding work there. Only my brother Issa at the age of four, my nursing baby sister, Susan, and I remained at home to help my father and mother in the chores of life. My mother worked like a man, perhaps even harder. She started to move about at the crack of dawn and did not stop working until the day had passed and everyone had gone to sleep.

Next to the hut, my father set apart an area within the large courtyard and built a low wall around it made of stones of different sizes, in the manner of the walls of the terraced plots. Behind this rocky fence, we raised three or four pigs which were insatiably hungry and which became fatter every day. My mother knew well how to prepare their fodder from leftovers, bran we bought in bags, and other ingredients. She asked me to record in one of my school notebooks the amounts we spent on buying the bran, the millet, and the other materials which the pigs needed, in order that we could be sure, she said, that we did not become involved in a trade as Juha did when he bought twenty eggs for a shilling and sold twenty-five for a shilling so that people would say he was a "merchant."

The most memorable day of my experience with these pigs was the day it innocently occurred to me that they had been imprisoned for too long in their pen, and I pitied them for having to lie languidly in mud and filth all the time. Why not let them go out to move freely in the open courtyard for one hour or two, then return to the enclosure?

That "noble" idea occurred to me when there was no one but me at home. I opened the door of the enclosure, entered, and pushed one of the pigs outside. I then pushed another and rushed out to the courtyard to ensure that, when the third pig came out, they would all remain within an area in which I could control them.

Suddenly, one of them began racing along the edges of the large courtyard (rejoicing in its freedom?), and it was followed by the two others. In turn, I ran toward the entrance of the courtyard, which had no gate, in order to prevent them from going out to the road. Indeed, this was exactly what came to their mind after three or four quick rounds, while snuffling and snorting and grunting.

When the first pig was about to fly past on its way out, I stood in its way; but it continued to advance toward me with its snout to the ground, and it darted between my legs. All of a sudden, I found myself sitting on its back with my face turned toward its posterior as it continued to run with me until I was flung off and saw all three pigs racing down the public road as if they knew where they were rushing!

I began to run after them and shout at them. Some of the neighbors and passersby realized my predicament, and so they ran after the pigs, caught up with them, intercepted them with great difficulty, and forced them with my help to return and enter the courtyard. From there, they suddenly became obedient and made their way to the door of the enclosure, one after the other. I quickly closed the door behind them and found myself trembling with fear and anger. What would have happened if they had escaped and were lost? Or was that the reward of doing pigs a favor?

My heart was throbbing, and I was out of breath. I felt terribly exhausted. I drew a bucket of water from the well and splashed handfuls of it on my face. The cold water refreshed

123

me, and I drank some. Then I went to the mulberry tree, climbed it, and sat among its branches. And I let my mind roam freely again in the vastnesses of the world.

✳ **14** ✳

When Yusuf left us and went to work in Jerusalem, he left at home most of the books he had bought with his own little money in the last few years. He had made a special little box to keep his books in, and it was tantamount to a treasure chest to me, for I returned to it from time to time in order to take out what I could read, everything being different from what we read at school. I continually referred to two books because of the variety and enjoyment they offered me: *Bahr al-Adab* (*The Sea of Belles-lettres*) and *Majani al-Adab fi Hada'iq al-ʿArab* (*Harvests of Literature in the Gardens of the Arabs*) by Father Louis Shaykhu, S.J.

Bahr al-Adab abounded with illustrated short stories, mostly about animals and birds, taken from Ibn al-Muqaffaʾs *Kalila wa Dimna* and La Fontaine's *Fables*, and each story ended with a pithy line focusing on its moral. As for *Majani al-Adab,* it took me at that early age to an amazing world of wise sayings, proverbs, histories, travels, and poems in a continuous summary that presented the ancient Arab experience in its most alluring and fascinating forms. The book was divided into chapters, and the text had all the Arabic vowel marks and other signs, so that it was not difficult to read. The names at the end of the selected passages enchanted me, such as al-Thaʿalibi, al-Qazwini, al-Shurayshi, Ibn Qutayba, al-Atlidi, al-Ibshihi, al-Ghazali, al-Masʿudi, Abul-Faraj, Ibn Battuta, Ibn ʿAbd Rabbih, and al-Tawhidi—uncountable names whose sweet and obscure resonance lingered in my memory until their importance became clear to me later on, in my mature years.

In a chapter entitled "On Current Proverbs" in *Majani al-Adab,* I read a large collection of Arab sayings, many of which I learned by heart because I liked them and read them repeatedly. Foremost among them was a saying I never forgot: "Two persons are insatiable, a seeker of knowledge and a seeker of wealth." I asked myself which of the two I was, and immediately decided I was a seeker of knowledge. Wealth to me was something unknown and did not concern me, but knowledge was in my hands with all its splendor in these books. When Teacher Jabboor asked us to write a composition entitled "What I Want to Be in the Future," I wrote, "I want to be a teacher, because I would then always be with books, learning from them for myself and for others at the same time." This was exactly the profession I chose years later with obsessive determination.

Among the books, there was the first novel my brother ever acquired: a translation of *Robinson Crusoe*. I remember the day when he first brought the illustrated book home and began to read passages to me describing how the ship that carried Robinson Crusoe was wrecked and how, alone among the passengers, he escaped death and found himself on the rocks of a desolate island. From the wreck of the ship, he began to build a hut, using his intelligence and effort, and he started a new life with the help of Friday, the only man he encountered on the island. This kind of endurance enchanted me and aroused delightful and obscure thoughts in me which made me hunger for more.

One of my school friends, who came from Bayt Sahoor, once brought me a book that made my mouth water as soon as my eyes fell on it because of its title and its numerous illustrations. Entitled *Siyar al-Abtal (Biographies of Heroes)*, its heroes had strange names: Achilles, Hector, Ajax, Odysseus, Theseus, Hercules, Persius, Andromeda, all heroes of Greek epics and myths. I begged my friend to lend me the book. But he said he only wanted to sell it. How much? Two piasters. How could I lay my hands on the amount of two piasters? He quickly took back the book from me. I begged him to bring it to school on the next day. That was a few days before Yusuf left us to work in Jerusalem. So I informed him that evening about the book and its beautiful illustrations, and I asked him to give me the money to buy it. He said, "I am saving money to buy Elias Anton Elias's *English-Arabic, Arabic-English Pocket Dictionary*. Its price is thirty piasters . . . don't tell Father or Mother about this . . . here, take two piasters from the amount I saved, and bring me the book tomorrow. . . . God will compensate me, perhaps in the book itself."

On the next day, I added *Biographies of Heroes* to my brother's collection, and it later found its way to the box of books and remained another one of my most exciting reference books.

In the box, I found a number of volumes of *Sirat ʿAntar (Antar's Romance)* and Bani Hilal's *Taghriba (Westward Trek)*. There were also detective stories, some of which were serials, like *Milton Top* and *Johnson*. Among the books was one that had lost its covers and its pages were in closely printed lines whose words were not vocalized; it had become a collection of yellow papers, which my brother bound together with pins. It was not easy to read at first, but as I turned the pages, my eyes fell on a title saying, "The Tale of Masroor the Merchant and his Beloved Zayn al-Mawasif."

After years of telling us stories every night and repeating many of them, my father's store of them had dried up. Furthermore, he began asking us to tell him something of our own readings. I thought to myself that I would read this tale and relate it to my father when he returned home from work in the evening. And lo and behold, in one fell swoop, I fell into a new magic circle when I read the following:

> It is narrated that in olden times and previous ages there was a merchant named Masroor, who was one of the most handsome people of his time. He was wealthy and lived comfortably, and he liked to go for walks in gardens and parks, and to entertain himself with the love of beautiful women. It so happened that he was sleeping one night and saw in a dream that he was in a most beautiful garden in which there were birds; among them was a white dove as resplendent as polished silver. That dove appealed to him and a great passion for it entered his heart. He then saw a large bird swooping

down and snatching that dove from his hand. This upset him immensely. He then woke up and did not find the dove. So he nursed his passion for it until the morning and said to himself, "I must go today to someone who would interpret this dream for me." And morning came upon Shahrazad and she ceased all permissible speech.

On the 787th night, she said, "I heard, O happy king, that when Masroor the Merchant woke up and began nursing his passion until the morning, he said to himself when morning came, 'I must go today to someone who would interpret this dream for me.' So he walked right and left until he was at a distance from his home. But he did not find anyone to interpret this dream for him. He started coming back home, and on the way, it occurred to him to pass by the house of one of the merchants. The house belonged to a rich man. When he reached it, he heard the sound of moaning emanating from a sad heart and singing the following verses:

> The breeze of the east wind blew from her camp's traces
> With a fragrance that would heal the sick on being smelled.
> I stood at the remains of her encampment and asked,
> When only the ruins could answer my tears,
> And I said, "Breeze of the wind, pray tell me
> Will happiness ever return to this house?
> Will I enjoy the favor of a deer whose tender figure
> And dreamy eyes made me languish for her?"

"When Masroor heard that voice, he looked inside the house and saw a most beautiful garden in which there was a red silk screen studded with jewels and gems, behind which were four slave girls. Among them there was a young woman of above-average height, who was like a shining full moon. She had black eyes, joined eyebrows, a mouth like King Solomon's ring, and lips and teeth that looked like corals and pearls. Her beauty, her figure, and her proportionate physique were bewitching. When Masroor saw her, he entered the house and walked on till he reached the screen. She raised her head and looked at him. Whereupon he greeted her, and she returned his greeting with sweet words. As he looked at her and contemplated her, his mind and his heart were enraptured. He looked at the garden full of jasmines, violets, roses, orange blossoms, and all kinds of fragrant flowers; he looked at the trees laden with fruits and at the birds which included sparrows, pigeons, nightingales, and doves, each bird singing its tune. And amid all of this, the young woman was swaying with her beauty, her figure, and her proportionate physique. . . ."

Although I found it difficult to read those entangled words, printed in Arabic without commas or periods, and without vowel marks and orthographic signs, they took me to a distant and enchanted world, teeming with colors and tunes and full of tall trees and sweet-smelling flowers, with birds and young women dallying among them. I could not distinguish between the former and the latter, and Zayn al-Mawasif offered me the most delicious food, and I played chess with her on a board of ebony and ivory and exchanged poetic verses with her, the like of which I never read in my school books.*

But I was irritated because I did not know what happened to Masroor and Zayn al-Mawasif after they began to play chess, for the following leaf was about eighty pages later and exactly one hundred nights afterward.

> On the 888th night, she said, "I heard, O happy king, that when the Baghdad man who owned the slave girl entered Basra, he became perplexed, for he knew nobody there and did not know where al-Hashimi's house was. . . ."

And yet I continued reading to the end of the story, where I reached a new title, "The Tale of Ward-Khan, Son of King Gilead." I flipped through the pages quickly, night after night, and suddenly I was going backward, for I found I was in the 580th night:

---

*Two or three years after that, I wrote my first story—and it was somewhat long, for it filled one of my school copybooks. It was about a man who dreams of a beautiful girl. In the morning, when he wakes up, he feels that passion had taken hold of him, so he paints her with oils on a large canvas so that her image may remain before his eyes and he may express to her his love in confidence. One day, he meets the sweetheart of his dream, and lo and behold, she looks exactly like the picture he had painted.

She said: "I heard, O happy king, that the old man, who was the remaining one of the ten, said to the young man, 'Beware and never open this door lest you repent when repentance is of no avail.' The old man's sickness then became worse, and he died. The young man washed him, put him in a shroud, buried him with his friends, and sat down in that place which was sealed off with all its contents. And yet, he was anxious and kept thinking of what the old men were about. One day, as he was thinking of the old man's words and his warning not to open the door, it occurred to him to look at it. He got up, walked in that direction, and searched till he found a pleasant door covered with cobwebs and locked with four steel locks. On seeing it, he remembered the old man's warning, so he turned away but was continually tempted to open the door. For seven days he resisted the temptation but on the eighth day he gave in and said, 'I must open that door and see what happens to me after that, for God's fate cannot be rebuffed and nothing happens without His will.' He got up and opened the door after breaking the locks. On opening the door, he saw a narrow corridor. So he walked in it for about three hours and suddenly reached the bank of a great river. The young man was surprised, and he walked on the river bank, looking right and left. All of a sudden, an eagle swooped down on him from the sky, picked him up with its claws, flew back into the air, and took him to an island in the middle of the sea. It placed him on the island and left. The young man was perplexed and did not know where to go. As he was sitting, he saw a sail looming in the sea like a star in the sky, so his attention focused on the boat in the hope that his deliverance would be through it. He kept looking at it until it came close to him, and he saw that it was a boat made of ivory and ebony, its oars were made of sandalwood and aloe, and it was all plated with glittering gold. It carried ten virgin slave girls as beautiful as full moons. When they saw him, they left the boat and came to him, kissed his hand and said, 'You are the bridegroom-king.' One slave girl as bright as the sun in a clear sky approached him, carrying a silk kerchief in which was a royal robe and a golden crown studded with all kinds of jewels. She drew closer to him, robed him, and crowned him. The slave girls then carried him to that boat in which he saw many kinds of colored silk carpets. Then they spread the sails and took off into the sea. The young man said, 'When I moved with them, I thought that it was a dream, and I did not know where they were taking me. . . .'"

I was sitting on the mat, and I heard the chickens and ducks cackling outdoors as I read. The words glowed in my mind; they glittered like gold and sparkled like jewels. I imagined myself walking on colored silk carpets spread over the waves of a wondrous sea of dreams, which brought me to a land full of soldiers whose numbers only God knew. They offered me five horses with golden saddles studded with all kinds of pearls and precious stones. I chose a horse and I rode it, and it moved in a procession among flags and banners to the beat of drums. When I reached a green meadow with palaces, gardens, trees, rivers, flowers, and birds glorifying the Almighty One, a king came and led me to the palace:

> On the 581st night, she said, "I heard, O happy king, that when the king took the young man, he walked with him in the procession till they entered the palace, the young man's hand in the king's. He seated him on a golden chair and sat by him. When the king unveiled his face, lo and behold, he was a slave girl as brilliant as the sun: she was beautiful, splendid, perfect, wonderful, and coquettish. She said to him, 'Be it known to you, O king, that I am the queen of this land. All those soldiers you have just seen, whether on horseback or on foot, are women. There are no men among them, for men in our land plow, plant, harvest, till the earth, build up the country, and serve the interests of people through diverse crafts. As for women, they are the rulers, the officeholders, and the soldiers.' The young man was greatly surprised at that. Then the queen turned to him and began to entertain him and alleviate his loneliness with kind words. She then asked him, 'Will you accept to marry me? . . .'"

At that moment charged with expectation, my mother entered having returned from the market. She put down her basket full of the tomatoes, zucchinis, and eggplants she had bought, and she shouted to me, "God bless you, sweetheart. Go out and draw a can of water for me from the well. It is time for making the dough. What's the matter with you? What are you thinking of? Come on, get up quickly!"

Those yellow leaves of the book remained a promise of mysterious, almost secret pleasure. I returned to them from time to time, and in spite of the wide gaps in them, I read what I could in some sort of sequence according to the numbers of the nights. I briefly related what I read to my friends, especially when we spent whole days secluded in the vineyards. In addition to what I read, I knew by heart many of my father's stories, and I enjoyed narrating them with many additions that my fanciful creativity suggested on the spot. I often returned home with a hoarse voice after such seclusions in the vineyards because of the great number of stories I told!

Yusuf told me one day how he came upon those leaves of the book of *One Thousand and One Nights* at Khugaz's shop, when he worked there. Every few days, Khugaz used to bring a heap of old magazines and copybooks, from which he tore out sheets to wrap what he sold. One day, my brother was using two old worn-out books and tearing pages from them, time and time again, to put a piece of halva on, or a quantity of olives, pickles, or dried fish before he weighed them and wrapped them. He noticed that some pages had strange pictures, and he read the explanations under them. He realized that they were long stories. When he looked more carefully, he realized that they were serialized in nights, and he guessed that they must be the *One Thousand and One Nights*, of which we had read selections in the *Majani al-Adab* reader. It was Saturday, the market day of the week, and their clients among the villagers and Bedouins were crowded at the door of the shop. Khugaz and Yusuf tore off the leaves and wrapped what they sold at a great speed. At an opportune moment, Yusuf hid the two collections of yellow leaves under another heap of magazines and newspapers when he noticed his Armenian boss was not paying attention. At the end of the day, he returned home with his booty, or what remained of it, and he began to read with such deep joy that he added it to his books, which he eventually collected in that little box.

One day it occurred to me to show these leaves to Sulayman Fathu, one of my closest friends since the time we resided in his parents' house. I began to read some of them to him when he snatched them from my hand and flipped through the pages. He could read only a few words in them, for he was behind in the second elementary class of the German School at al-Madbasa and used to play truant whenever he could deceive his elder brother, especially after his father's death. I wanted to take back the leaves from him, but he insisted on taking them outdoors with him and said, "I want to read them in the daylight." He headed for the pigsty and looked down on it from the top of the stone enclosure.

I followed him. At that moment, the pigs had thrust their heads in their manger and were gobbling the bran dough and the vegetable peelings which my mother had filled it with. Suddenly, Sulayman tore off some of my dear leaves and threw them into the pigs' manger. . . . I flew into a rage and tried to snatch the remaining leaves from his hand, but he threw them all in the direction of the pigs from the top of the enclosing wall. They fell down and scattered under their feet, while Sulayman burst out laughing with joy at what he had done.

I opened the gate of the enclosure and rushed in. I began to shove the rump of this pig and the buttocks of that, in order to save my leaves from being trodden upon, but the pigs were heavy, and I could hardly move them. I saved what I could of the leaves, while Sulayman continued to laugh, shout, and clap his hands behind the enclosure as though he was watching a comic scene he had created.

He was surprised when he realized that I was seriously angry. I refused to speak to him, so he said, "Are you angry about a collection of leaves from an old book? By God, I can't understand!"

I answered, desperately looking at the soiled and torn remnants in my hand, "He who throws leaves like these to pigs will never understand, of course!"

I did not care that he then turned his back to me and said, "Well, I'm going then." He crossed the courtyard slowly, hoping that I would ask him to stay. But I wanted him to go away so that I could go back indoors with my leaves. I now only had a few, and the page numbers were far apart and had lost their sequence. I had to admit they were no longer of much use to me. And yet, I returned them to the box of books in spite of their small quantity and miserable condition.

That was another early experience which recurred in my later life whenever I was inattentive: you give some people a pearl, thinking that you offer them an experience of a unique intellectual pleasure, but you are amazed by seeing them throwing it to the pigs with determination, boasting of their blindness and rejoicing in their stupidity.

However, Sulayman was innocent, and it gave him great pain to know he had committed an error, the real nature of which he did not know. For he and George came to me that afternoon, and he apologized and tried to make some conciliation. We then went out together to Father Anthony's Monastery. The friendship among the three of us continued for many years, even after our paths diverged and distances between us increased.

 15

Toward the end of our second year of residence in Jahluqa's house, my father left his job as gardener at the hospital because of his inability to continue working. Not only did he suffer from pains in his left leg, but he had also become unable to control its movement except with difficulty. His left hand trembled, and he could not stop its trembling. The hospital doctors and nursing nuns did not neglect him, for they gave him several kinds of medicines, but they all failed to cure him. Sister Janine was the most sorry that he had to quit working for them.

After the failure of the doctors, those who seized on my father's treatment were two or three illiterate persons of the many practitioners of "Arab medicine." Some of them wandered about among the houses, calling out like any other peddlers,

"Arab medicine, folks! An Arab physician, folks!" Those I saw were usually Bedouinlike and came mostly on Saturday, the market day of Bethlehem, when the town was crowded with people coming from all over. Each of them usually carried a bag containing little bottles and old cardboard and tin boxes full of dry herbs, fragrant powders, and pills of sugar, flour, and pepper. And they claimed these were their healing drugs.

I saw one of them at our house talking to my father and reviling the "civilized" physicians and their pharmaceutical drugs. He said that they were ignorant persons who fleeced people and that he alone, with his tried Arab medicine, could heal my father and relieve him of his pain. His opinion was that the healing treatment would only come through cauterization.

My father agreed to the cauterization, and this "physician" performed it in stages. First, he repeatedly cauterized him with a skewer on parts of his leg and back. My father bore the pain silently, hoping a miracle would happen. The burnt flesh healed after a while, but no improvement followed. Every time the physician came, he took his fee in advance before even saying what his next stage was. He then prescribed air-sucking cups, and days passed with those cups being repeatedly stuck to my father's back, sometimes accompanied by blood letting to remove "bad blood," until the skin of his back was impressed with overlapping circles left by the cups, making it look like a sieve for a long time. Then, one day, the man said, "Now, Abu Yusuf, I've come to you with the last remedy, after which you'll forget all your pains, return to your physical strength, and become as sprightly as a horse."

He took out of his bag a large, iron key with a black circular handle big enough to fill one's fist, and he said, "I am going to cauterize the calf of your leg with the handle of this key. After that, you'll thank me for the rest of your life and praise God a thousand times because He guided you to me. But tell me, do you have enough money these days?"

My father called out, "Maryam, give me my purse."

My mother did not believe in these swindlers, but she knew how much my father suffered, and she understood his desperate clinging to this last straw of hope (and what a straw!). So she did not want to argue with him, and she gave him his purse. He took out one or two pounds and handed them to the physician, as I watched what was happening with anxiety and fear. Some hope moved in my heart that this physician might succeed where the others had failed or that he might succeed this time after he had failed previous times.

He asked my mother to light the Primus kerosene stove and raise its fire to the highest intensity. He then put the handle of the key on its raging blue flame and waited.

We waited with him. He drank a cup of coffee. The waiting continued for a long time. All the while, the handle of the key was getting hotter, then red, then redder and redder until, after about one hour, it glowed like an ember.

My father pulled up his trousers and uncovered his left leg as he lay on a thin, matted rug with two pillows behind him. The physician picked up the key, holding it by its smaller end with a collection of rags to protect his fingers from the heat, and he applied the glowing handle to the calf of my father's leg. A plume of smoke rose with a horrible smell of burning flesh as he held the handle to the flesh of the leg and continued to hold it there. My father gasped sharply and breathed heavily with a rattle as he twisted, but he refrained from uttering a single cry of pain. However, a scream shot out of my throat against my will, and another came from my mother's throat as she shouted, "Ouch! Woe to me!"

The physician put the key aside to let it cool, some particles of flesh still clinging to it. He carefully looked at the deep, bloody brand on my father's leg and said, "Good news, Abu Yusuf. In two or three weeks, you'll get up like a lion. Yes, by God. But look here, good folks. The wound should not be allowed to heal in an unnecessarily short period. As soon as you find that it has begun to heal, thrust a few chickpeas into it so that it may become active again. Repeat this operation two or three times until the cauterization has its healing effect on the nerve. Good-bye and peace be with you!"

He then got up like a lion, picked up his key, and left. My

father remained lying on the floor for many days. Finally, when the wound began to heal, he insisted on following the physician's advice. He made my mother bring him some chickpeas, and he himself placed them on the red, inflamed flesh and pressed them and covered them with the bandage, thus causing the renewal of inflammation and pus. He repeated this disgusting operation, and several weeks passed, but they brought us nothing but disappointment and despair.

We did not see the face of the physician again. And I don't know how that hideous wound healed, looking as it did like a gaping mouth in the leg muscle. Yet, in spite of everything, it healed in the end and left a large, round scar as big as the handle of the key. My father, however, remained as sick as he was earlier.

In those days I wrote a play, having been motivated by factors I was not aware of at the time. I was fond of acting, especially after I had seen many plays at Father Anthony's Monastery and at the Franciscan Convent of the East. The Arab tales and the translated detective stories I avidly read created in my mind a teeming universe, which I did not fully understand, though it excited me and seemed to be full of intrigue, conflict, and murder in addition to much love that was not always the truly triumphant element. My father's sudden downturn, after the cauterization of his leg in that grim manner suggested to me that he might become the victim of a deception which we all did not understand, and that his death might cause the misery of his children; and yet he was heroically struggling before his death to ward off that misery. Perhaps this idea was what made me write my play about a father who dies and leaves a fortune to his three dispersed sons; there are, however, three enemies who covet that fortune, but they don't exactly know where the father has hidden it, and they want to steal it before the sons get it. Conflict between the two sides begins and leads to the death of the three villains.

I knew that my father owned nothing in this world other than the clothes on his back. But he owned his songs and tales, and his love that flooded everything around him. He owned his bodily strength, which had begun to abandon him, and he owned his spiritual strength, which would never abandon him. I never heard him utter a word of abuse, and he wanted me to be like him in this regard. He had faith in God that was never open to doubt, whatever suffering he might experience; and he had trust in people that was never shaken, whatever cunning he encountered. He sought nothing from God but His satisfaction, and he sought nothing from people but that they refrain from harming his family. Was this the treasure which, in my boyish mind, was transformed into a fortune that an old man hid for his children, while his enemies waited for an opportunity to steal it from them? Who knows how the mind of an eleven-year-old works, as he sits under the mulberry tree or among its branches and looks toward the distant blue mountains where heaven and earth meet, and so he imagines that humans and angels meet, perhaps devils too, and he writes a play about the conflict of good and evil? Did I want to clarify to myself how the angels of good and evil try to deceive each other or plot against each other in their endeavor to possess the soul of man, which perhaps is the real treasure? Was I compensating for the incapacitation of my father who lay down on the floor like an oak tree that the winds had felled but that had earlier defied all the winds of the world?

One afternoon, on my return from school, I saw my father standing at the door after his wound had healed. He was observing my mother as she faced the blaze of the clay oven, according to her custom once or twice a week, and fed it with the flattened lumps of dough and after a while retrieved hot loaves of bread from its inner wall and piled them in the trough. Leaning on a stick for the first time, my father contemplated her as her face turned red like the loaves and as the sweat poured from her forehead and down her cheeks. Suddenly, he said to me, "Come, let me give you a puzzle to solve."

I asked, "And what if I solve it?"

He said, "You won't."

"Give it to me, then."

"A tantalite bowl, lined with pearls and covered with copper. What is it?"

"A pomegranate."

"No, not this time. It's not a pomegranate."

"It is a pomegranate, Dad. You've lost!"

"This tantalite bowl which is lined with pearls and covered with copper is your mother. Yes, it's your own mother, whom you see over there, being roasted at the door of the oven. Look carefully. Outwardly, she is copper, exactly. But inwardly, she's full of pearls and rubies and gems."

He then fell silent, and I saw two tears welling up in his eyes. I knew how much he loved hot bread, so I ran to my mother and took a loaf from the trough saying, "Mom, my father says you are the sweetest pomegranate in the world."

She said as she retrieved one more hot loaf and laid it on the pile of loaves, "Ah, make fun of me as you wish . . . pomegranate, indeed!"

She then carried the piled-up trough and followed me into the house. As my father and I were chewing the delicious hot bread, she spread out the loaves to cool on the rattan mat in the corner, and the room was filled with the aroma of this "blessing," as my father and mother called our daily bread.

I said to my father, "Today, I am going to give you a new puzzle to solve."

He said as he broke another piece from his loaf, "Give me whatever you have."

I said, "Dishes following dishes, from here to Khuraytoon. What are they?"

He answered laughingly, "You think you can outwit me now, don't you? They are the tracks of camel pads. I wish only that you could have seen the camel caravans of old as they left traces of their pads in the soft earth . . . dishes following dishes. Ah, for the days of yore! Well, here is another puzzle for you."

I said, "Give it to me."

He said, "It has crooked horns and black eyes. She-goat it is, may God not guide you to it. What is it?"

My mother yelled from inside the house, "What are you doing, Ibrahim? Making fun of the boy? Don't you have a harder puzzle?"

I said, "Thanks a lot, Mom. It is our own she-goat with its crooked horns and black eyes, isn't that so, Dad? But I've prepared one puzzle for you out of the deep."

My father said, "Give it to me."

And so we continued to exchange puzzles till we were tired.

I had to draw water from the well, water the plants, feed the sheep, and collect the eggs laid by the chickens and ducks—all before dark. I also had to play with my brother Issa and amuse my sister, Susan, as Fulla shared our play and amusement. I had then to turn to my school duties and do my homework in the light of the lamp, which my mother would have filled with kerosene and cleaned by removing the previous night's soot from the glass.

My mother prepared supper as I turned the pages of my copybooks; then I saw her carry in the coffeepot and a cup. She sat by me on the floor, while my father leaned on his pillow. She poured some coffee for herself (my father had been forbidden to drink coffee), and she said as she took a sip from her cup and appeared as though she was suddenly carried on a cloud that took her away from us to some place we did not know:

"The days of yore . . . your father remembers the days of yore . . . I swear by your life, we saw nothing but woe in them."

I asked her, "Do you remember those days well?"

She took one more sip from her cup and said, "Remember them? Those before the war? Those after the war? I always try to forget them."

A wave of memories carried her away. My father helped her, and she helped him to recall some of that past, which appeared to me to be very remote and about which my father often said he was happy because his children did not know it.

Murad was a baby seven or eight months old when his father, Dawood, my mother's first husband, and her twin and only brother, Yusuf, were both killed on the same day in 1909 in tragic circumstances. My mother was then a young woman seventeen years old. She wore black in mourning for her brother and her husband for four years (as did her mother, my grandmother, Basma). Then one day, my father appeared in her life, and "he

139

captivated her," as she said, with his height, his handsome looks, and his dashing character. He was only one year older than she was, and he said to her, "Take off your black clothes, lady, and you shall never again wear them after today. . . ."

On the day he married her, he promised her and said, contrary to custom, "If our firstborn is a boy, I'll name him Yusuf after your brother. As for the second, I'll name him after my father. Are you satisfied?"

My mother said, "I took off the black clothes, thank God. But the war soon came, and they took away your father as a soldier . . . oh! The days of yore . . . we saw nothing but woe in them."

Here, my father asked me, "Tell me, what do the books of history that you and your brother read say about the woes of the days of yore?"

I realized, then, that my father had suddenly given me a question that was much larger than myself. Being at a loss for an answer, I said to him laughingly, "Daddy, I don't know the answer to your puzzle this time. Give me an easier one, and I'll give you the correct answer!"

16

Mount Khuraytoon lies a few kilometers east of Bethlehem. It is a distinctive mountain, visible almost from all parts of the town. From our house, it appeared as though it were lying down to rest exactly in the middle of the horizon, full of mystery, with its violet conical shape whose upper half had been cut off (perhaps that is why it acquired its Arabic name, which means conelike). At that remote distance, it looked like a clay oven or a large ground oven. When the sun rose, it sometimes seemed to rise from the mountains' depths like a golden loaf.

The mountain had another name, al-Furdays, and this made me imagine it was a real Firdaws (Paradise) waiting for those who would go to it to find happiness. But Teacher Faheem simply said it was only an extinct volcano, one side of which could be easily climbed, leading to its broad summit; from there one could descend to its inside where, among the volcanic rocks, one could see the remains of an ancient palace that went back more than two thousand years. The teacher suggested he would take the students of the fourth elementary class on a trip to the mountain on the morning of the following Friday, so that we might penetrate its mysteries and explore its secrets, if any.

At dawn on that Friday, I got up from bed with great enthusiasm. My mother prepared boiled eggs and bread for me, and she added some leftovers from supper the night before. She put all that in my school bag, which I hung from my neck by the strap. I rushed out to school where the students—about thirty boys—had gathered. Under the leadership of the teacher, we set out and took the road that descended toward Bayt Sahoor first, then began to climb gradually to a rocky area with no roads, except for the traces of tracks made by animals. Beyond that, there was no trace of a road or path of any kind.

At first, there were a few neglected and thin trees at some distance apart, from which one or two birds flew to soar into the air then return. From time to time we saw some thorny bushes, whose names we did not know, gushing forth from among the rocks. A little beyond, there was no trace of any plant, and we did not see a single bird. We continued to walk amid the rugged stones and thorns as the sun rose and began to shine in our faces; then it climbed over our heads, and shone with a strange harshness. We continued to enjoy the merriment that Teacher Faheem aroused in us by his comments and jokes. But Mount Khuraytoon, our promised paradise, was farther away the more we walked toward it—or so we felt. Then the thirst began.

Three or four boys had brought little felt-covered canteens with them, from which they and those near them drank until the water ran out. As for me, I imagined that, despite my thirst, I would need no water before we reached there. The teacher assured us that, on the mountain, there was a well whose water was as cold as ice. So I waited.

Merriment decreased; then our conversations sagged. Perspiration increased and sweat flowed. There was no shade of a tree or a rock among the stones. The teacher urged us to hurry up, alternately moving between the front and the rear of the line of boys, encouraging everyone and constantly joking.

My friend Adil Asali was walking in my company.

He suddenly asked me, "What's in your bag?"

I said, "Eggs, bread, and. . . ."

He asked, "Don't you have oranges?"

I said, "No. Do you?"

He said, "I have one orange. Are you thirsty?"

"Very."

"Me too."

He took out a large shiny orange from his bag. The teacher saw him and ran toward him saying, "Wait, Adil. There is a long way still in front of us. We'll soon reach a cave. Keep your orange till we reach the cave. Do you see that hill over there?"

The sight of the orange, then its disappearance, increased my thirst and Adil's. The boys began to repeat, "We're thirsty. . . . Is there no well in this area?"

After great effort, we reached the cave promised by the teacher, and we took refuge in its cool shade. Adil took out the orange and peeled it. The sharp smell of spray from the rind refreshed me. A few boys surrounded him, each expecting a part of it. He divided it into sections and distributed those to them. I got one and he another. I placed it in my mouth and began to squeeze it slowly between my teeth, swallowing the juice drop by drop—how sweet it was! Never in my life had I tasted a sweeter piece of fruit than that little, fragrant section from Adil's orange.

No sooner had we resumed walking than I found that the pleasant acidic sweetness that I had savored in drops in my throat began to make me even more thirsty. We walked, stumbling on the rocks. Our throats, tongues, and lips were getting drier. The sun was increasingly hot and more intense. And across the bright sky, three black ravens soared, swooped down over our heads, then rose upward and disappeared behind us.

We began to hurry up as much as we could in those circumstances. The teacher encouraged us, "We're almost there, we're almost there, young men! Ilyas, pull yourself together! And you too, Shukri! Jabra, where is your determination, man? . . . We're approaching . . . Adil, don't you have another orange? It's not necessary. Take heart, young men. He who endures will triumph."

Adil and I exchanged looks. I imagined that we would soon fall down, all thirty of us, on our faces, on the sharp rocks, under the rays of the sun, and that we would all slowly die of thirst. We did not find a single plant or flower under our feet to comfort us. We went around the hill, and before us rose another hill that looked down at us from its high rocks with hostility, as though wanting us to remain thirsty until we died.

At that moment, I saw Shukri weeping and saying, "I'm thirsty." Another boy cried, then another. I felt a strong urge to cry like them, and two burning tears rolled down from my eyes, and I sobbed. We walked, stumbled, and were exhausted. I imagined we were going to die and that our families would never know what happened to us, unless the ravens told them of our fate.

Suddenly the hill before us revealed a soft, rocky slope; and as soon as we descended it, we saw at a distance the mouth of a well made of rough stones arranged in a circle with a rusty iron cover in the middle. We ran to the well and raised the cover, shoving one another, as the teacher was trying to control our impetuous behavior lest we fall into the well. "A bucket, folks! Look for a bucket!" There was no bucket anywhere. The surface of the water was two meters down, or less, and we were almost dying of thirst. But the teacher was quite resourceful, for he emptied the two-vessel travel bowl he had in his bag and shouted, "Let everyone wearing a belt undo it!"

He gathered a few belts, tied their ends together to form a rope, then tied its end and the end of another belt to the two ears of one of the vessels, and let it down into the well. He then raised the water which he had been promising us during our hours of torment. We drank, one by one, each thinking he would drink the entire well. The water was fresh, despite visible impurities, and it was as cold as ice, as the teacher had said. Or was it thirst that suggested that to us?

High rocks surrounded the place like giants. We took refuge in the shade of some of them, sat down on the ground, and took out the food we had brought. Only then, as we were eating, did we begin to look at the scenery in front of us and all around us, and feel the breeze that was gently blowing on our faces.

At a short distance from us was the trace of a path beaten by feet over the centuries and spiraling to the top of Khuraytoon. The high fortress above our heads was no less enticing. Between its rocks carved into the shapes of mythical beasts by erosion (as our teacher explained) were the entrances to the caves that looked like gaping jaws shouting and inviting us to climb up to them and explore their depths. We found a crack leading upward to one of them. Despite the crevices which we had to jump across with daring and alacrity, we made our way upward clinging to the slippery rocks until we encountered a cave whose entrance looked like an arch or a door constructed by a human hand sometime in a past age, welcoming those wanting to enter. One of the boys said, "This is the door of the maze! My father told me about it."

On entering its shady and cool depth, we found two adjacent and similarly arched doors. Many of us were afraid to enter, but some of us, including myself, boldly went through one and some through the other. Each door led to more doors, each of which took us to rooms or hollow places with doors. It was as if the place had been prepared for a strange game we did not know, but we wanted to play.

The few boys divided themselves up and streamed through these ramifying entrances, in which darkness was becoming thicker and thicker, and we began to separate from one another. Finally I found myself alone with Adil, and our rush slowed to a walk. We stayed together groping our way cautiously in this dark stone forest, seeking greater depths as the openings branched out in all directions like tunnels. Suddenly we became aware that the place was getting intensely damp and dark, and we no longer heard the voices of our friends. A strange hum seemed to come to us from the black depths. The ceiling above our heads was low and full of protrusions and we could not see what our hands or feet touched. We had indeed entered the labyrinth.

Adil was holding on to my shoulder when we both fell down on the ground. We were terrified.

"Let's go back!" Adil shouted. "This is the cave of the demons, I know."

"Yes, but how are we to go back? Give me your hand."

I got up, pulled him up by the hand, and turned around, hoping to see a glimpse of light that would mark the correct direction for us. I was frightened when I saw nothing but pitch-black darkness. Adil's grip on my hand tightened. I felt the dryness of my throat all over again.

With some guidance from instinct, we groped our way, but the darkness did not end. I was scared and felt suffocated. I said, "It seems we shall either die of thirst or of suffocation."

He said clinging to me, "It is your fault!"

I said, "Okay . . . but stay with me."

It seemed we were indeed going back in the right direction, but we passed through doors we had not gone through before. In the distance, a weak light loomed and guided the direction of our walk. It was important that we avoid any diversion through doors that might lead us away from our destination. Then we began hearing the voices of our friends, and finally, we went out into the bright sunshine.

The students were standing at the entrance waiting for us. The teacher counted them again and again in order to be sure that no one was lost in the labyrinth. Adil and I were the last to come out. The teacher scolded us for our foolhardy courage. I said, "Courage? By God, we almost died of fear!"

My heart was still throbbing violently, and I could not calm it down.

After this, we descended quickly shouting and racing one another, as though we had been set free from a terrible prison. We ran toward al-Furdays. Climbing up to it was easy and effortless after the difficulties we had endured.

Its circular top was open to the sky. We ran down to the interior, strewn with volcanic rocks, among which were huge chiseled stones indicating the ruins of an ancient palace. The teacher said it was the palace of King Herod the Great. The Romans had installed him as king over Palestine thirty-three years before the birth of Christ. When he heard Jesus was born in Bethlehem, and he could not find him because the Virgin Mary and her fiancé Joseph had fled to Egypt with him, he ordered that all the newborn babies in the town be killed. This was the horrible massacre that came to be known as the Massacre of the Innocents. Herod had hoped that among them he would kill this baby who, he was told, would be a danger to his life and kingdom if he were to live and grow up. Herod had killed several members of his own family, even some of his own children, in order to keep his throne. Why not kill the children of others? But he died the same year. Herod Antippa was his grandson and the king who ordered that John the Baptist be beheaded. He was also the one who, before death, saw his fat body being eaten by worms and, with its stinking odor, attracting ravens from the farthest regions to perch in croaking flocks on the balconies, windows, and doors of his palace waiting to have their banquet of his flesh and fat. . . . But his palace was in a place other than this one that was open today to the splendor of the sky.

As we were leaving the ruins, we said, "We have had a good look at history today, and what a history. Let us bid it good-bye quickly!" We descended running toward the well again, we drew some of its water, and we drank as we prepared ourselves for the return.

The return was easy; what a miracle! We took a path other than the one by which we had come, and we realized that in the morning we had taken the wrong way and were lost. Now the path was clear and less rugged and stony. It did not take us half as long as it did in the morning, and no one was thirsty this time.

When I arrived home after sunset, exhausted and hungry, I looked at Mount Khuraytoon, now distant and merging with the blue mountains on the far horizon and illuminated by the remaining colors of the setting sun. I felt a sudden joy overcome me as I looked on, trying to understand something very insistent: After a trip of suffering, had I imagined I caught a glimpse of Paradise? Or had I rather visited the Kingdom of Death and returned from it with a greater zest for life? Or were such imaginings more complex than my boyish mind was able to deal with? It never occurred to me that the experience of thirst to the point of death and the experience of the labyrinth to the point of terror would leave in my soul and my memory a deep impression that would stay with me in the coming years of my life and that would generate images and forms which I could know nothing about at that time. No doubt, I had intuitively guessed them, but I did not have the power to define or analyze them.

 17

On the edge of the Valley of the Camel and a little lower than the level of the New Road, a huge azarole tree towered up gracefully and was visible from our house situated on the hill above. The slopes of the valley were full of olive trees wherever one looked, but this wild azarole tree seemed to pride itself on its height, its expanse, and its towering grandeur. No one knew who planted it, and perhaps it burst out from the earth between two big rocks at a time nobody remembers. We used to see it clearly from the road, because its higher branches rose above the edge of the road. It swayed with every breeze as if beckoning to us, inviting us deliberately. We had only to climb up a rock or two, jump to one of its branches, then climb into its thick network of branches and leaves and fill our pockets with its sweet, yellow, little fruits.

In the season when olives were picked, we made it our point of entry to the trees of the valley. The harvesters, with sticks and ladders, picked the olives with a skill that went back thousands of years, and they sang merrily. "ᶜAla dalᶜuna" was the favorite song of everyone and the valley was filled with it as soon as the autumn arrived, and the harvesters, men, women, boys, and girls, sang it as they shook the trunks and branches, beat them with their sticks, and reached the higher and more inaccessible ones with ladders, making the green olives fall like pearls on the red soil. They picked them up in handfuls and filled the baskets and bags. They moved from tree to tree, and their songs and the tunes of the double reed and the flute moved with them. Whatever time of day it was, there was always someone, perhaps visible to us and perhaps not, who played the double reed or the flute, sitting on a rock somewhere and pouring forth his continuous tunes which echoed in all parts of the wide valley like flowing whiffs of a gentle breeze.

Some olives stubbornly clung to the branches here and there or remained hidden among the pebbles and in the cracks on the ground lined with stinging nettle or various kinds of autumnal anemones. Schools being off for a few days to permit students to participate in the picking of olives, we took our school bags and gleaned behind the harvesters; that is, after they had left the tree, we picked the stray or stubborn olives they had missed, however few, these being free to anyone who found them, and we put them into our little bags. When our bags were full, we returned to our lonely azarole tree, if there was anything left of daylight; we climbed it, and we too sang our songs, happy with what we had reaped.

I tried to understand the meaning of the Bedouin words of "ᶜala dalᶜuna" and I took pleasure in the uncommon ones among them. I liked to imagine how the "north wind" changed the color of lovers; and I saw them dark, tanned by the sun that highlighted their large, kohl-painted eyes which were intensely white and deeply black as they shone and glittered, while the north wind blew on them and increased their darkness—and their sweetness:

ᶜAla dalᶜuna, ᶜala dalᶜuna
The north wind has changed my color.
I'll write to my sweetheart on blue paper

And send many greetings to the beloved girl.
But, my girl, if you're intent on separation,
Come, talk to me on the telephone.

I tried to imagine the voice of this beloved sweetheart as she lisped on a telephone. I had once seen a telephone at some people's home but had never put its receiver on my ear. Many years later, when I spoke on the telephone for the first time, this song and these words were the first thing to come to my mind. And I wished that the speaker on the other end of the line was that beloved girl intent on separation from her lover, whose story I heard as I picked olives in the Valley of the Camel and filled my pockets with azaroles; for then, I could ask her, "Why, pray tell, are you intent on separation?"

■ ■ ■

I was returning from the azarole tree and going home with Sulayman. Near the tree, a lane branched out from the New Road and went upward for some distance ending with the garages of the Bethlehem buses, whose company had been recently established. At that point, the lane turned and connected with Ras Iftays Street as it continued upward. Our house was on the high ground above this lane, which actually used to be the original road leading to Jerusalem for many centuries, until the New Road was built and paved in the early 1920s. Without going through the old town, the New Road led directly to Manger Square by skirting the edge of the valley in a large arc.

One of the owners of the garages at that turn of the lane was a man related to us called Abu Ilyas. After my father left his job at the convent hospital because of his sciatic nerve disease, he used to go to Abu Ilyas sometimes in order to amuse himself and talk to the workers there, who were two or three men of his acquaintance. He contemplated the motorcars being repaired, for their complexity and motion enchanted him, and he used to say, "This is the kind of work I always wished I did!"

One day Abu Ilyas suggested to him, "Why don't you work for us?" When my father said he had grown too old to learn a new trade, let alone that he was sick, Abu Ilyas insisted that my father would be allowed to help the workers only as much as he could. The wage would be very small, one shilling per day.

My father agreed despite my mother's objections. My brother in Jerusalem did not know what was happening at home. I, too, objected as much as I could because I was afraid my father would definitely be harmed by the exertion. But my father insisted, and said the job was easy and would afford him some pastime.

No more than a few days had passed after he started working at the garage, when Sulayman and I were returning from the hospitable azarole tree and going home uphill. I saw my father, busy with a number of tires he was carrying from the sidewalk to the interior.

I said, "Let me help you, Dad."

"No, no," he said. "Go and play with your friend."

I said, "Let me carry these tires with you, and then I'll go home." Turning to my friend, I added, "You go. I'll follow you later."

Sulayman left, and I helped my father.

A few meters below us, there was a car lifted on a jack so that a front tire could be installed. One of the workers had already fitted the tire on the iron rim of the wheel and had pumped air into it. He asked my father to carry it to the car.

I volunteered to carry it myself. I held the tire and found it was heavy. So I stood it up, fully inflated and tight as a football. Instead of carrying it, I thought I could roll it. In fact, I had only to push it a little, and it rolled along easily in front of me.

I ran after it, nudged it once or twice, and it started to roll downward at a faster pace. When I tried to push it sideways toward the car lifted on the jack, my hand hardly touched it, and it continued to roll in the direction it chose for itself.

I ran faster behind it, but it outstripped me like an unruly horse, and it increased its speed down the road as I continued to run after it with all the strength at my command. I saw it going farther and farther in front of me as I panted behind it, unable to overtake it, and it looked like an enraged animal that had been released from all restraint. In those moments, there was a man peacefully riding his donkey up the road. I was afraid the crazy tire would collide with him and throw him and his donkey to the ground, but it violently glanced off a stone sideways and bounced in the air two or three meters, then landed on the edge of the New Road. I hoped it would fall on its side, and its flight would come to an end. Instead, the cursed tire stayed upright, bounced again, and rolled with greater force toward the azarole tree. I continued to run and pant, unable to grasp the meaning of what I saw, and I heard my father shout at me from a distance, "Now, look what you've done! Look what you've done!"

On the edge of the valley, near the azarole tree, the tire bounced once more, fell into the depths of the valley, and disappeared from my sight.

In turn, I jumped to the edge and caught sight of the tire rebounding from one rock to another with tremendous force as though it contained a genie that Hell had released. I was frightened. My God! When is it going to stop? When will this cursed tire stop?

From one retaining wall to another, the crazy tire began alternately to come to earth and fly, bouncing its way down the terraced slope of the valley and, by some cunning miracle, it did not collide with the olive trees, as if it knew that they would put an end to its craziness. I was seized by a terrible alarm and felt as if I had committed a horrible offense, from which there was no salvation for me.

My father caught up with me, just as confused as I was, his eyes fixed on the spiteful tire. I felt that the tire was treating us unjustly by that satanic flight. I feared that the owners of the garage would require my father to pay for it, and he would be unable to pay and would thus be obliged to work for them for nothing because of what his reckless son had done.

Suddenly the tire hit an olive tree at the bottom of the valley and, from our distant position, we saw it fall and disappear. My father was faster than I was, and he leapt like a leopard from one rock to another and shouted in my direction, "You stay where you are, so that I won't lose my way . . . do you hear me? No, don't come down. Stay where you are. . . ."

In a instant, my father regained his youth and agility. He took my position as a point of reference in his descent, for it was easy to get lost in that large and deep valley. It seems he had drawn an imaginary line tracing the movement of the tire in its successive jumps beginning from the place where we were standing. I continued to observe him as he descended the terraces, looking up in my direction from time to time until I could see him no more. I despaired and said it was impossible; he would never find the tire.

However, he reappeared a short while later. After some time which I found to be an eternity, I saw him very far away, waving to me.

He did not rest for even a moment. I saw him raise the tire and begin his ascent. I did not hear anyone singing at that hour, nor did I hear the tune of a flute or a double reed. The valley appeared to be desolate, dreary, and oppressive. My father carried the tire, heavy as it was, and climbed up from stone to stone, from rock to rock, alternately appearing and disappearing.

Finally, I saw his head rise near the friendly azarole tree, amazingly proud. He was panting and sweat ran down his face. The tire in his mighty hand was like a brass bottle which he had returned the genie to and imprisoned him.

I rushed to him, and he saw the tears flowing from my eyes as I was shaking uncontrollably. He patted my head with his free hand and said, "Don't, man! Isn't it a shame? I'm your father, and you can always depend on me!"

When I tried to take the tire from him, I was surprised that he was still able to laugh. Yes, he was able to laugh and joke with me, the offender who was seized by alarming imaginings, and he said, "What? Do you intend to let it fly once more?"

He gently pushed me with his hand as we made our way upward back to the garage and he said, "Quick, now. Go home. No more of this work or this nonsense. Go and study, and sing ⁽ᶜ⁾ataba."

I hesitated as I looked at his eyes and his big black mustache. His forehead was straight and broad, his cheeks were full and shining. He appeared to me to be a towering and beautiful giant, like the azarole tree that I liked. He never raised his hand to hit me, whatever I did, and he never shouted at me in anger. In those moments, he looked to me as a young man again, radiating strength and vigor, in spite of being exhausted.

That was the last time. In the evening, he came back home, and pain returned to demolish him with its evil stubbornness. Youth began to leave him quickly, though he was only in his late thirties. The vitality he exhibited when he sang lessened, and he no longer danced with his friends at weddings. He told fewer tales until he said one day, "From now on, it is your turn. You will sing to us, you will tell us tales from the books you read, and you will be the ones to shake the earth with your friends when you dance."

18

The last part of 1931 and the beginning of the following year were unhappy for us all. Emphasizing his independence, my brother Murad got married in the early part of the year to a woman he himself had chosen, without much enthusiasm on the part of our family. He rented a small room for himself and his wife on the top floor of an old building at the entrance of the Municipal Market. Nine months later, he was blessed with the birth of a baby who, however, did not live more than four or five months, and its death cast the first tragic shadows on my brother's life and on the life of the rest of the family.

Furthermore, Yusuf was not happy with his tedious work in Jerusalem. When he came to celebrate Christmas with us, bringing with him my grandmother whom we now got to see very rarely, a quarrel broke out between him and my mother, perhaps because he failed to offer her the amount of money she had expected on that occasion. This spoiled the festive mood at home and ended with anger, screaming, and weeping, and Yusuf returned depressed to Jerusalem with my grandmother.

As the rains came and the cold became more severe, we

realized that our life without some income had become quite difficult with my father still sick. We sold the sheep, we sold the chickens and the ducks, and we sold the pigs.

School to me, with its students and teachers, its books and atmosphere, was an escape and a refuge, like nature. I did not find it strange, as the principal did one day on noticing that, during about three years, according to his records, I had not missed a single day on account of laziness or illness.

In those days, I had begun to draw in pencil, then in colors. Near the Zarrara Arch on my way to school, I used to see a barber who had set up an easel next to the barber's chair in his shop. On it he had placed a large canvas on which he had drawn squares in which he had sketched lines in pencil; then, slowly and carefully, he added colors. Whenever I passed by him, day after day, I saw the picture developing on his canvas, for he worked on it in the long intervals between one client and the next. I used to stop at the door and watch him, and he encouraged me to observe him closely. He explained to me that the painting was an enlargement of a postcard-sized photograph of a man and his wife. On the photograph, he had drawn little squares, and he placed it next to the canvas to copy from; then he added to the canvas the oil colors he chose, which were mostly bright and joyful with red and blue dominating.

And this was what I did too, but in pencil. Our school textbook, *Modern History of Europe* by Muhammad Izzat Darwaza, was full of portraits of historical figures. I started to make enlarged copies of them in squares, and I was particularly proud of an enlarged picture of Napoleon that I made. In spite of the poor printing of the pictures, they made me consider how eyes and lips were formed in pictures, and I realized how difficult it was to draw noses in a convincing way if the face was in frontal view, and how much more difficult it was to draw hands and feet. I concentrated on trying to perfect their shading and shape, and I intently observed people's eyes and lips, and their hands and feet in various movements and circumstances, and I began to see in them a beauty that fascinated me more and more.

In a flurry of enthusiasm, when my mother looked at some of my drawings, she said, "I'll give you one piaster to buy

coloring pencils, on condition you draw our house with them."
She did not know what a challenge she had innocently set up for
me by giving me those ten coloring pencils in a cardboard box.
It was not long afterward that I discovered watercolors and
obtained a box of them with two or three brushes. Watercolors
remained my medium of drawing after that, along with the lead
pencil, until I went to study in England—seven or eight years
later—where, at last, I taught myself how to paint in oil.

Drawing was another door through which I entered a world
in which I could find a necessary refuge and a means to pleasures that shielded me from a great deal of misery later on when
the walls of home closed in on everyone inside, and there were
no openings in them from which scenes of trees with birds or
views of mountains and valleys laughing in the melting sunshine
could make their way indoors.

In accordance with Yusuf's proposal, it was decided that the
family move to Jerusalem, to a house recommended to my
father by some of our acquaintances there. Having just finished
the second school term, I informed Teacher Jabboor of that,
toward the end of March 1932, and he made me obtain a transfer note to the Rashidiyya School in Jerusalem from Principal
Fadeel Nimr. The transfer note included a list of my recent
marks and information that I was the second in class, had no
absences, and so forth.

I was sorry to leave the school I loved and the teachers and
students among whom I felt warmth and security. I was appre-
hensive of going as a stranger to a new school in a large city
where I would be as lost as I once was.

On the morning of a heavily clouded day, a large truck
came to the road near the entrance of our house's courtyard.
We began to move onto it our bedding, mats, bags of provi-
sions, cans of olives, copper utensils which were our mainstay
for cooking and washing, the cans we needed to carry water,
and the large water jar which always occupied the most important corner of the house. The dearest things I myself carried
were the chest of books and our beloved cat, Fulla.

My father sat next to the driver, and the rest of us huddled
among the heaps of belongings: my mother, my grandmother

(who had come to help us in the moving operation), my little brother, Issa, my baby sister, Susan, and myself.

In about half an hour, we were in our new neighborhood, Jawrat al-Unnab, which was situated in an area below the level of the main road, just before reaching Jaffa Gate. Above it and above the road, the western wall of the city rose majestically with David's Citadel and the minaret of the Citadel Mosque, both among the famous landmarks of Jerusalem (a few years later, I was to paint them in watercolors and the picture was one of the most beautiful I ever did). Yusuf was waiting for us.

When the truck stopped near a large house with two floors above the lane, I hoped the room my father had rented was on the top floor. Instead, we entered an alleyway near the stairs, and at the end of it, we came to a landing from which a flight of stone stairs led us down to a courtyard with the basement rooms. On the opposite side across the open courtyard, there were three more rooms with a tin roof, and behind them was a tall house with a window opening toward us (after a year or a little more, my relationship with Khalil Dajani, the boy living there with his family, would become strong). Behind and around this house were many other houses. Our "new" house was one of the two rooms on the ground floor in the alleyway. To the right of the door was a small window, blocked by a wooden board that had once been painted blue, and it opened on what looked like a chicken coop, which was one meter wide and separated from the courtyard by a flimsy net fence. We put a wooden box outside the door, and it soon became the bench we used whenever we wanted to sit at the edge of the court-yard in the fresh air, and it also became another container for the books and magazines that kept accumulating. A few days later, we decided to cut a new little window into the top of the wall opposite the door, and its sill was exactly at the level of the road on which the building stood. If it brought us much dust through the fine metal screen, it also brought us some west wind that kept us from stifling (or decreased it), especially when we closed the door at night.

In every room of that building, there was a family with

many members. Although there was a well in the middle of the courtyard with a pulley in an arch above it to carry the bucket, we found out that the well was full of brackish water that could not be drunk. The neighbors reassured us that, near the building, there was a "spring" that received its water once or twice a week in accordance with an arrangement with the Jerusalem Municipality. All we had to do was to buy from it the water we needed at the times allotted to our neighborhood.

Suddenly I found myself thrust among a large number of women, men, and children and in constant daily contact with endless noise and tumult.

In the room with the tin roof opposite us, there lived a family hailing from Bir Zayt and consisting of a widow (who immediately made it known to us that she was the landlord's sister), her son, Mansoor, and her two little daughters. Mansoor was about fourteen years old. He was the first one I asked about the location of the Rashidiyya School in the morning after we had settled in our dark room. He said, "I'll take you to it myself. I'm a postman as you see from the uniform I'm wearing. I know the area of Herod's Gate quite well."

He accompanied me on the way to Jaffa Gate, and through crowded arched streets, we came down to Bab Khan al-Zayt and the Spicers' Market; then we walked in open narrow streets covered with cobblestones. We ascended to the inner square of Damascus Gate and went out from that magnificent high portal and walked eastward along the city wall to Herod's Gate. Mansoor shouted to me as he pointed across the road, "Do you see that sign?"

On it was written in large letters "Al-Rashidiyya Secondary School."

After I thanked my guide, he left me and I entered the wide gate below the sign. I walked in a passageway lined with trees in the middle of the playgrounds. I was confused and anxious and unsure of what I would encounter. When I reached a wide flight of stone stairs that took me up to a beautiful verandah shaded by a graceful tall pepper tree, my confusion and anxiety increased.

From the verandah, I entered a large hall on both sides of which were the classroom doors, and behind them I could hear the teachers' voices. Someone took me upstairs to the upper hall and to the principal's room at the farthest end. In my hand, I held the most important document I had known in my life up to that moment, the transfer note.

I knocked on the door, which was actually open, and a young man, seemingly the principal's secretary, came quickly to me from the opposite room, and he asked, "Yes? What do you want?"

I gave him the note, and he read it and smiled (I later learned he too was from Bethlehem, from the Nastass family). He led me in to Mr. Arif al-Budayri, who was sitting behind a large desk piled with files and papers and surrounded by shelves lined with books.

The principal here was entirely unlike the one at the school I had left: he was a man with a grim look, a big and bald head, a fat face, and a rather corpulent physique. He had sharp eyes and a piercing voice, and it was evident he also was a man who could command obedience and make decisions. He took the note from the secretary's hand, read it, and said without smiling, "When did your family move to Jerusalem?"

I said, "Yesterday."

"Well," he said, "if you had been late, we would have dealt with you differently!"

He laid the note on the desk, got up, and said, "Come." He led me to the fifth class, a nearby room on the same floor, and we entered. A teacher was teaching Arabic, and the room was radiant with daylight coming from two large windows. The teacher said at once, "Rise!" The students stood up with the usual rattle.

The principal said, "Husayn Afandi, this student comes to us from Bethlehem. We hope he will be able to continue with us."

He turned to the boys standing and said, "Sit down!" He then went out, having given me the impression that I might not be able to continue with them.

I sat on a seat near a boy, who whispered to me as soon as

the principal had left, "My name is Hisham al-Nashashibi. What is yours?" Then Mr. Husayn Ghunaym asked me the same question, and after I answered him, he said, "These are your classmates: Abdallah al-Rimawi, Mahmud al-Bahsh, Ghalib Hadaya, Sharif al-Khadra, Tahir al-Budayri. . . ," and he named all the students, about twenty in all, or a little more.

As I was noticing his little flat nose and sharp voice, he said, "Are you good at Arabic?"

"Perhaps," I said shyly.

"Come up to the blackboard," he said.

I went, my knees shaking. I held the chalk with my fingers.

He told me to write two lines of poetry: "And when I saw that Mount Bishr had come between us / And pangs of yearning had pierced my heart. . . ."

I wrote what he dictated while he carefully looked at the words I was writing; then he said, "Now, analyze this verse grammatically."

I began to read the words slowly in order to understand the meaning. A number of students raised their hands saying, "Sir, sir. May I analyze it?" It seemed they considered me to be too slow, and it is possible they had analyzed it earlier for the teacher. So I began: "*And*: conjunction. . . ," and I went on. The students fell silent and the teacher commented on each word I analyzed saying, "Yes . . . correct . . . correct. . . ." I was not sure about the last word, but I ventured a grammatical analysis of it, and the teacher shouted, "Correct! Great! What do you think, Abdallah?"

I realized that Abdallah al-Rimawi was the cleverest among the students and that the teacher was particularly interested in his opinion. I returned to my seat, having regained my confidence. I sat up straight in my seat and, now reassured, looked around to enjoy seeing my new classmates.

When the class ended and the teacher left, the students gathered around me in the five minutes preceding the next class, and they asked me about my marks, my rank in class, where I lived, why I had left Bethlehem, who my father was, and whether I had any brothers. Ghalib, the class prefect, tried to reduce the noise and threatened to write the names of those causing trouble on the blackboard.

The bell rang and a strikingly tall, young teacher entered, named Yasin al-Khalidi. He was elegant in his white suit. He had thick, shiny black hair which he parted on one side and combed behind his ears. He was a very handsome young man, very much like a cinema actor. His long, delicate fingers attracted my attention as he turned the pages of the English book he used in this class. He noticed that I was a stranger, so he approached me and asked who I was and where I came from. Then he posed the question I feared:

"What English textbook did you study?"

I said, "*New Method Readers.*"

"Yes," he said, "but what volume?"

"Volume 3," I answered.

He said, "Aha! Do you know what volume we read here? Volume 5. How can you follow the class with us? What do you think of going down to the fourth class?"

I said, "No, no. Impossible, sir."

He said, gesturing with his long-fingered hand, "But you will not be able to follow the class in volume 5."

I begged, "Try me, sir. Try me for one month."

Yasin Afandi chuckled cutely and said as though he was resigning himself, "Okay, we'll try you for one month. Only one month. But what if you disappoint me?"

"If I do, kick me out of the school!" I answered unhesitatingly.

He then began to walk among the students' desks and teach us a new lesson, pronouncing English in a wonderful way I had never heard before.

It was his habit to surprise the students from time to time with a short, written test or quiz, and I was not accustomed to that. Yet, in the following days, I did not prepare myself for any other class as well as I did for his lessons and his tests.

Did I disappoint him after a month? He entered the classroom, took out the list of marks from among his papers, and shook his head as he contemplated it. He laughed almost inaudibly with surprise and said, "Folks, we have wronged Jabra. So what did he do? He has earned a place ahead of you all. His mark with me this month, believe it or not, is 95. Take care, Abdallah. Who is first in English this month? Jabra . . . congratulations."

Abdallah al-Rimawi was the first student in class in all the courses. He did not like the fact that I had "snatched away" this first rank from him, at least in one course. When we went out to the playground, he said to me that the matter was a mere coincidence and that it would not happen again. He was frank and friendly at the same time. I admired his intelligence and diligence; however, I could not help noticing that he was too self-confident and ready to quarrel at any moment with the older boys as well as with the younger ones. I was later surprised that we never fought with each other, neither that year nor, indeed, in the five years following that we spent together in the same class. Whenever I took the first rank away from him in any other course later on, even in the monthly examinations, the teachers were frank in blaming him or in reproaching him as they cautioned, "Abdallah, take care. . . ."

I liked all my teachers at the Rashidiyya School, but no one of them ever cautioned me about other students competing with me. They were more inclined to caution Abdallah about other students competing with him, especially about my competition. But I did not compete with him and certainly did not want to be above anyone else. All I wanted was to secure success so that I would not "fail" and would not be expelled from school before I obtained a piece of paper enabling me to work as a teacher in some school in order to help my family with the salary I earned.

What I was really obsessed with was the reading of books, school texts as well as others. I filled my brains with Arabic and English words, with dates and events, and with diverse information which, as time went on, began to assume a certain pattern that had its own intellectual dimensions and gave me real pleasure. It was this pleasure that consumed me despite my young age. Whether a person was ranked first, second, or tenth in class was not something that bothered me or aroused my interest. And this is exactly what Abdallah realized later, though he continued to "take care" by studying harder and reading more widely. In spite of his many wrangles with students and teachers in the following years, he and I remained on good terms until the end—until we both graduated with degrees in secondary education from the Arab College at the beginning of the summer of 1937.

I was pleased, even in that fifth elementary class, by the fact that one of the teachers was of a type I was not accustomed to. He was Wasfi al-Anabtawi, who taught us geography. During his class, he talked to us about his experiences in England, France, Egypt, and other countries. He did not look in the book as he taught us but dictated to us pages and pages of knowledge that seemed to flow spontaneously from his deep learning. A graduate of Oxford University, he was tall, very elegant, and put a handkerchief into his sleeve at the wrist. He was very kind, but sometimes very harsh when angry; then his eyes shone like lightning behind the lenses of his gold-rimmed glasses, and everyone fell silent out of fear. He spoke an Arabic language in which classical Arabic was mixed with the dialect of Nablus, emphasizing the velarized q which Jerusalemites rarely pronounce. He controlled our minds and imaginations, and I don't think that anyone was ever distracted for a moment from what he was saying. Whenever he explained a difficult point, he repeated his favorite phrase, "But what does this actually mean?" And he clarified the point again in a different manner.

The history teacher was Diya al-Khatib. A graduate of the University of London, he was a friend of Wasfi al-Anabtawi but totally different from him, for he was rather short and neglectful of his appearance. He spoke with no extravagant eloquence as though he considered speech to be the maximum of meaning in the minimum of words. His language retained strong traces of the dialect of Hebron, the town which he originally came from. And he never lost his composure. His mastery of the materials of his course made us listen to every word he said. I felt he opened amazingly ramifying temporal depths in my way of thinking as much as Mr. Wasfi opened amazingly broad spatial horizons.

Hasan Arafat taught us arithmetic and algebra, and in later years he taught us physics. He was a graduate of the American University of Beirut. He too came from Nablus originally. He was distinctively short but he had a remarkable presence with the mathematical logic and considerable accuracy of whatever he said, which he emphasized with peculiar gestures of his hands when holding a pencil, chalk, papers, or books. He had a keen sense of humor, and made us laugh though he only smiled slightly, nothing more, and raised his eyes sideways until we ended our laughter.

One of the teachers I liked most was Jamal Badran, the drawing teacher. He spoke in an Egyptian dialect as a result of his education in Cairo. Because he was engrossed in his art, he spoke as he drew or as he corrected our drawings. In two or three months, he taught me basic principles of drawing, especially the rules of perspective and shading, that have continued to guide me in my studies and art work all the years of my life. He loved a joke but also loved discipline, and so he alternately made us laugh and treated us severely. And since he had a deep passion for Islamic decorative art (he was famous for decorative engraving on leather), he taught us the rules of decoration in addition to drawing from life. At his request, we went to the Holy Sanctuary to copy parts of the arabesques on the walls of the Dome of the Rock, and we drew them in our art books in lines and color. My companion in those beautiful afternoons spent in the vast space of the Dome, the structure which I loved at first sight, was Sharif al-Khadra who, like me, was fond of drawing; he later specialized in the decorative crafts at one of the art institutes of Cairo. The large courtyard, of which the Dome of the Rock occupied the middle, inspired awesome peace and tranquillity after the noise and tumult of the neighborhoods we crossed on our way to it. And whenever I left the Dome of the Rock to go home, I left peace and quiet behind me there and returned to the heart of things throbbing with the clamor of human beings.

19

Peace and quiet at home were briefer and more difficult to obtain among all those denizens of the courtyard and the upper two floors. Clashes of will took place, mostly among women, concerning the most trivial matters: clotheslines, the cleaning of the communal toilet, the smoke from the fires kindled in the corners, water splashed in front of the doors, children's squabbles. But harmony somehow always returned, though only temporarily, because it was a necessity of life; it came back with reconciliation and kisses and cups of coffee.

The widow, Umm Mansoor, was often the cause of the trouble. The fact that she was the landlord's sister gave her the idea that she should interfere in the tenants' affairs, although her brother disapproved of that and told her so in front of them. In the room next to her house, Abu Latif lived with his wife, Umm Latif, and their daughter, Naᶜima. Naᶜima was a girl of my age, with rosy applelike cheeks. Every morning she wore a black uniform with a white collar and went to St. Joseph's School. Abu Latif left after her, carrying a boot-polish box to shine shoes. He always looked exhausted, even at the beginning of the day, because of his advanced age. His one-eyed wife stayed at home, and from behind the glass of her window looking out on the courtyard, she watched everyone coming and going.

In the evening, I sometimes saw Naᶜima through the window pane as she lit the kerosene lamp. The light shone on her face in the middle of the darkness as she hung the lamp near the window, her eyes large and dreamy, her plump lips half open, and she looked out at the dark courtyard, perhaps knowing that I was standing at our door staring at her and not wanting her to move away from where she stood.

Next to them, at the other end of the courtyard, lived Abu Yusuf al-Aᶜraj (The Lame) and his wife. "Al-Aᶜraj" was his surname, he was not really lame. He was a blacksmith who normally spoke very little. He was rather short and stocky, and had no interest in the affairs of the neighborhood. In contrast, his wife, Rafiʿa, who was taller than he, never ceased talking to all the neighbors in the absence of her husband. On certain evenings, Yusuf would come back home late from work; he'd stagger down the stairs in a merry mood. He'd sit by the door of his house and sing, and Rafiʿa would bring him more *arak* and appetizers, and drink a glass with him, "Only for your sake," she would say. Resuming his singing, Yusuf would suddenly stop and begin to complain in a loud voice about the hardships of his job and the difficulties of life. He would then revile his relatives one by one, and then curse the whole bloody world and everyone in it. For some reason, he'd suddenly start to beat his wife, who would scream and run into the house, her loud weeping heard all over the courtyard, until some good neighbors volunteered to reconcile the couple. The evening would end with Yusuf himself bursting out weeping, and so his wife would embrace him and try to pacify him, but he would resist until he finally stopped weeping and, with his head on her breast, fell sound asleep.

Opposite their house, in the room similar to ours in the basement floor of the building, lived Latif—the son of Abu Latif—with his wife and his three daughters: Georgette, Yvette, and baby Odette. I did not know where Latif, who was a house painter, had come up with all those French names, until I learned that his wife, Sultana, had been brought up at a girls' orphanage in one of the French convents in town. The oldest of the girls was nine or ten years of age, with blond hair and blue eyes, and she accompanied her aunt Naʿima to school. But her mother constantly needed her to help with the house chores and take care of the other two girls, especially Odette whom she always carried and held to her breast. And this disturbed her regular attendance at school.

Latif showed an interest in me when I showed him a copybook in which I was busy writing my first long story. With the exception of my brother, he was perhaps my first reader: for he read my story as soon as I had rewritten it neatly and drawn a picture for its cover, and he came back to discuss it seriously with me. Its title was "The Lady of Dreams," and most probably its subject was a mixture of ideas drawn from *The Arabian Nights* and the Pardaillan novels of Michel Zevaco (translated by Tanyus ᶜAbduh), of which Yusuf and I had read many. A year or two later, I gave the story to his daughter Georgette to read, and she never returned it, not even when her family left the neighborhood, and so I lost all traces of the girl and the story.

There were two doors facing each other at the top of the stairs leading upward from our lower courtyard to the alleyway that led one to the entrance of the building on the main road. The door on the left led to a narrow balcony overlooking the lower courtyard, and its railing was lined with cans planted with geraniums and basil. The balcony belonged to a room in which two unmarried sisters lived. They always sat on the balcony and, through the flower cans, watched the goings-on in the lower tenements, and they were hardly ever heard making a sound. One day, one of the two women "kidnapped" me, literally. She waited behind the door and as soon as I reached the alleyway after climbing the stairs, she abruptly opened the door and pulled me in by the hand, laughing. She seated me on a long bench along the balcony railing, near the sweet-smelling basil. She told me that her name was Salwa and her sister's was Hannah. She asked me about my family, and I secretly wondered what accounted for this sudden interest in us. Then she brought me a letter and asked me to read it to the two of them, for they were both illiterate, although their appearance suggested otherwise. I read the letter to them in spite of its bad handwriting, and I reread it. Then Salwa brought me a pencil, tore off a sheet from a copybook, and asked me to write an answer to the letter on their behalf.

I took the paper and pencil and asked, "What shall I write?" She said, "Begin, first."

"With what shall I begin?" I asked.

"Well, with the usual greetings," she said, "then on to the main subject."

So I wrote: "From a long distance we write, and with a yearning that cannot be measured. If you ask after us, we are in the best of health and in the happiest state of mind, thank God. We lack nothing but the news of your happiness and the sight of your sweet and beautiful faces. . . ." I continued for four or five lines in this manner with many rhyming clichés, which I then read to the two sisters. They were delighted and asked for more of the same until I said, "Sorry, I have no more memorized greetings left."

Hannah said, "Well, this will do. Now, to what we want to say in the letter. . . ."

I gathered, despite their circumlocution, that they were negotiating with their correspondent the marriage of Salwa but without being very explicit or specific. The matter subsequently required many more meetings and letters, and each time I read a letter to them and answered it on their behalf, Salwa made me swear not to tell any one of my family or the neighbors about the subject. In the end, everyone learned that the two sisters left the neighborhood because Salwa got married to a man from Ramallah and took her sister with her. And I was the only person who had actually followed the affair in all its phases.

Meanwhile, Musa al-Khuri, his wife, Maryam, his mother-in-law, and his two sons moved in to the room opposite the two sisters at the top of the stairs. He too came from Bethlehem, and the elder of his two sons was as old as my brother Issa, so they became friends at play and school. Musa was related to my father, though rather distantly. We became more closely related: when my sister Susan was baptized, his wife acted as godmother to her.

Musa was a stonecutter who dressed building stones. A chip once flew off a stone he was dressing, hit the corner of one of his eyes, and almost blinded it; but he regained his sight in what he considered to be a miracle, and always remained concerned about his eyes. Although he was illiterate, he was fond of political discussion and followed events as reported by others, especially those who read newspapers. I noticed that he went every Sunday to pray at the Church of the Holy Sepulcher, and that he spent most of the time in its courtyard where the men gathered and talked about matters in general, and in particular about

167

developments in the Palestine issue. He listened carefully and discussed matters with a lot of enthusiasm. He used to buy a newspaper every Sunday morning; he would give it to any young man in the church's courtyard who appeared to him to be literate and ask him to read the headlines aloud and possibly some other items, especially the editorial. He returned home with the newspaper folded in a rectangle and shoved into the side pocket of the jacket he wore over his long silken *qunbaz,* the name of the newspaper, *Falastin,* looming large over the upper edge of his pocket. When he saw me or my brother, he gave us the newspaper to read to him items the others had not read.

He said to me one day, "Do you know, Godson, what I have wished all my life?"

And before I tried to guess, he added, "To learn how to read! I carry a newspaper in order to make people believe I am a newspaper reader. Imagine!"

I asked, "And why don't you learn how to read?"

He said, "I'm afraid that they would say that I went to school after my hair turned gray."

I said, "First, you are still young. Secondly, I'm ready to teach you, if you accept me."

He did not believe what I said, and he asked, "Honestly? Do you think you can teach me how to read at least the newspaper?"

I said, "Let us try. And let us begin today. Where is your newspaper?"

From that day on, I began to teach him how to read. In addition to the newspaper, I used his son's primer written by Khalil al-Sakakini, which began with *ras, rus* and *dar, dur,* and he was quick to learn the first principles of reading.

When we moved to a more advanced kind of reading, and I required him to study at night, he began to show signs of fatigue and said, "To tell you the truth, Godson, I return home exhausted from dressing stones all day, and I have no energy left to concentrate on anything . . . and, you know, my eyes are not as good as one would wish."

I suppressed my ambition to teach him further, and he was content with the fact that he could now read the headlines of his favorite newspaper. He might sometimes venture to read the editorial as best he could, and he understood it in his own way, perhaps more by context and reading between the lines than by understanding the meaning of every sentence. The important thing was that he now bought the newspaper and read it to himself or to his family without having to resort to others.

■ ■ ■

Until that time, we had been unable to possess two basic things: chairs and a clock. Our table, necessary for studying if not for other purposes, was a *tabliyya,* a round and low wooden table about one foot high, that my brother had made in Bethlehem when he first learned carpentry. It was stowed away in a corner of the house, standing on its edge. When meal time came, we rolled it to the middle of the room and sat around it. After we finished eating, my mother cleaned it, and we rolled it back to its corner. But now, we started the practice of moving it to one side after supper, and after it was cleaned, I put my books and copybooks on it and studied and wrote my assignments. Sometimes I drew or tried to write a story while sitting at it. But I could also write and draw in the manner of the ancient copyists, sitting on the ground with one knee up to prop my copybook on. I also sat down cross-legged with a wide board of wood in my lap which I used as a table, or I lay down and wrote in my copybook directly on the floor. Yet, the *tabliyya* was best because I could put the wretched kerosene lamp on it at night, and thus my pages and the room were illuminated at the same time. And woe to me if I raised the wick more than my mother thought proper, for she would remind me of the cost of kerosene that the lamp consumed every day, and she complained, "O Lord, when will You save us from this kind of living, and from this soot and horror."

In Jawrat al-Unnab, there wasn't a single tree to which I could escape to be by myself with my books. There came a time later when I discovered a nearby field just beyond al-Shamma'a, on the hill overlooking the Jawra from the west side. It had a few olive trees and rocks, and wildflowers grew all over it; I used it as a private retreat. I doubled my efforts at the new school in order to prove to the principal and teachers that I could follow the lessons of my class in spite of my coming from a school they considered to be rural, far off, and below their standard. I therefore sat at my low table at night, surrounded by family members and guests from the neighborhood and elsewhere, and I tried to study amid the noise, the gossip, and the laughter as though I belonged to another world. But I realized that, if I wanted to do my homework properly, I had to get up in the small hours of the night before dawn, while everyone was asleep, in order to study as I should. I therefore decided to go to sleep early, at about nine o'clock or a little later and get up at three in the morning and benefit from the two or three hours of silence preceding the beginning of day for all the other residents of the neighborhood.

We did not have a clock to tell us when it was time to get up. So my father volunteered to wake me up at the time I wanted. In the Old City of Jerusalem, there was a famous convent near New Gate named the Terra Sancta, and it had a high conical belfry with a large clock on each of its four sides; it struck the hours and could be heard all over the city, especially in the relatively nearby areas in the silence of night. The problem was that it struck the quarter-hour, the half-hour, and the three-quarters of the hour without striking the hour itself until, of course, the hour was complete. My father used to wake up at some time in the night, go out to the courtyard, and wait. If the clock struck the quarter-hour, he did not know what hour the quarter was after. So he waited to hear the half-hour, then the three-quarters of the hour, and finally the hour, before the clock announced it was two o'clock. He had then to wait one more hour. He was afraid of falling asleep in the meantime, so he walked about in the yard and had a drink of water, but he did not smoke—for had he smoked, he could have perhaps whiled away the time to ease the weariness of waiting.

He waited and remembered events from his childhood and his youth, and the terrible suffering he experienced as a military draftee in the Ottoman army during the First World War until he heard the Terra Sancta clock strike three. He then woke me up and went back to his bed. I splashed cold water on my face, washed my eyes, then brought down the kerosene lamp from the hook on the wall and placed it on my table. I did not raise its wick too much lest I should disturb the sleep of the other members of the family, and I studied until dawn. I went out to the courtyard afterward and continued to study in the light of daybreak, walking back and forth.

During examinations at the end of the school year, I often got up at one o'clock in the morning in an effort to gain a really good command of certain subjects. (This was how I prepared myself for examinations in all the subsequent years of my education.) On the day preceding the last day of the examinations, I heaved a sigh and said to my father, "Tonight, I will sleep until morning. Wake me up at six, if I am not up by then."

He said laughing, "Why? Are you tired and beginning to be lax?"

I said, "The subject of tomorrow's examination is religion. I am not required to take it. But I will go only to register my presence."

The religion teacher was the principal, Arif al-Budayri. Because Christian students at the Rashidiyya School were few, they had no one to give them religious instruction, contrary to the situation in the National School of Bethlehem. Instead, they were rather asked to go to the playground while their Muslim classmates received instruction in religion. The religion marks in the trimestrial and final examinations were not added to the total of the marks, and so they did not affect the student's actual rank in class. Those who did not take the religion examination were given mark estimates on this subject based on their conduct and behavior at school.

Arif al-Budayri was an educator who was famous in his field. Especially interested in the conduct and behavior of his students, he was strict in this regard and showed no leniency with anyone who broke the rules he himself set for everybody. His punishment was severe, consisting, among other things, of beating students with a cane on their palms or their posteriors. If the students respected and feared him greatly, the teachers themselves respected and feared him even more, as we noticed.

I went to the religion examination unconcerned. Like the other students, I went to my seat in the hall. The principal saw me empty handed while my classmates were busy answering the questions set for them. After about an hour, I was bored with sitting in my place without writing. So I quietly withdrew from the hall and returned home, not realizing the anger I aroused in the principal by that "horrid" deed of mine.

The summer holidays began and I was free; I was free at least from the cares of endless study and nocturnal assignments.

 **20**

I did not set foot on the school premises for the duration of the summer holidays, but I remained in touch with some of my school friends and especially Sharif al-Khadra, united as he and I were by our common love for drawing. He visited me, and I visited him in his home in the area of Bab al-Silsila in the Old City of Jerusalem.

The summer holidays for me were hardly a period of rest. Our house in Jawrat al-Unnab was one of many in the middle of a neighborhood, part of which was being transformed into an industrial area. In the vicinity, there was the Sultan's Pool, my wonderful place of escape, which still retained some collected rain water among its rocks. At the end of the day, I escaped to its blue water, where I felt as though I was sailing through the waves of the sea. On the elevated ground of its banks was held the Friday Market, which was crowded on Fridays with people buying and selling and with sheep, horses, and other animals. I hardly missed a Friday without going there with Sharif or with other friends in order to watch—and draw.

Nearer to us than the market and the pool was a street almost next to our house, on both sides of which were newly built shops for craftsmen. Each was a complete workshop, and most were blacksmiths' shops whose continuous hammering filled the neighborhood with additional din all day long. There was a carpentry shop too, and my brother Yusuf began to work in it. On the top of the sloping street, there was a small foundry that was one of the rare factories of its kind in the city. My father got acquainted with the founder and, despite his increasing sickness, occupied himself with trading with him in scrapped lead, zinc, and copper. He introduced me to the man, whose name was Bishara, and the man said to my father, "Why don't you send me this son of yours tomorrow, and I'll teach him a craft that is little known in this city?"

We agreed that I should work for him, but only during the summer holidays. My wage was two-and-a-half piasters per day, that is, fifteen piasters per week. And so, I spent most of the days of that summer making molds in moist sand and lighting the fire of the hellish furnace to smelt zinc, copper, and iron in the company of Master Bishara and his helper, "Prince" Yusuf.*

The master was a young man and quite skilled in his craft, which he had learned from the Germans at an orphanage they ran and made into an industrial school widely known in Jerusalem by the name of Schneller, the man who had established it. Bishara was strongly built, his shirt almost bursting with his wide husky chest and brawny muscles. If he was in the mood, he worked hard and quickly; but after a night of drinking, he was not enthusiastic about doing any work, so he spent the day among the sand molds and metal heaps in a state of lethargy and loss. The middle-aged "prince," who took

---

*In my short story "The Gramophone," published in my collection *Arak . . . And Beginnings from the Letter Z*, the reader will find many minute details about this period of my life which I will not repeat here; the reader will also find an evocation of some of the atmosphere in which we lived in those days. The story was translated by Denys Johnson-Davies and included in his book *Modern Arabic Short Stories*, Oxford University Press, 1967.

pleasure in telling the story of how he acquired his title during days of "glory" he spent in Cairo in the prime of his youth, used to respond sympathetically to his master's state: he was active if the latter was, and he turned to idle talk and daydreams when his master was sluggish and lay on the sand. Between the two of them, I tried to use my time as best I could.

Bishara's uncle was the real owner of the foundry and visited us every two or three days in order to deal personally with the clients and those with interests to be served. What he feared most was that his nephew would hand over the finished products to the clients and receive their payment himself. For Bishara would then go, in no time, to one of two places: either to a tavern where his drinking companions were waiting for his money or to the house of a certain woman whose daughter he wanted to marry and on whom he recklessly and uselessly spent what he earned—or what he saved after his expenses on *arak*. The gray-haired uncle came to the foundry in his elegant suit, and when he did not find Bishara in his place, he immediately set out looking for this "prodigal son," who had no consideration whatsoever for his uncle. More than once, I saw him bring his nephew back to the shop, and I saw Bishara staggering along, dragging his feet, red eyed and unable to see his way. The uncle scolded him and shoved him violently toward the sand heaps, and Bishara fell down on his face and did not get up. The prince and I tended to him after the uncle had left, and the prince enviously said, "Oh, how I wish for a state of drunkenness like this one!" The master remained in that condition all night long after we left the foundry. When we returned the following morning, we saw him as a young man who was lively again; he shaved his beard, washed his head and face with soap, and regained his cheerfulness and determination. After he dried himself with an old rag, he said, "Come on, folks! We have a lot of work to do today!"

The prince was worse than his master, for he had no uncle to keep track of his capricious behavior and mend his ways. His old clothes were so dirty one could not tell what color they were. The shreds he called trousers were held together by a miracle but did not always succeed in covering his private parts. Yet he was well spoken and had a melodious voice, despite the cigarette stubs he smoked. When he sang, we listened to his singing, and one of the blacksmiths from the neighboring shop responded in admiration, "Allah! Allah!" And so Yusuf sang his song more loudly so that all the workshops could hear it, and he stopped doing the work at hand. Even Bishara himself often exclaimed at such moments, "Damn you! How wonderful you are!"*

■ ■ ■

The summer days passed, and I continued to wait for the school report to be sent to me by mail as the administration had promised. But it did not arrive. July passed and August was about to come to an end, yet the report had not arrived. All kinds of suspicions began to come over me. I saw Sharif, and he showed me his report. He had passed and was to be promoted to the sixth class. I thought perhaps I had not passed, and so the report was not sent to me; or maybe it was sent and lost in the mail; and it was possible that the address I had given the administration was not correct. I could do nothing but wait for the holidays to end and the new school year to begin.

---

*I feel I should mention here what happened to Bishara a few years afterward. He had closed his small workshop, no longer visited us at home, and disappeared from the neighborhood. Early in 1939, as I was on my way home from the Bakriyya School where I was teaching that year, a beggar accosted me near Jaffa Gate, stretching out his hand to me as though he knew me. He was Bishara in an old *qunbaz,* walking heavily, his temples and chin bound with a dirty bandage. He was pale, unshaven, shifty eyed, and hardly able to talk. I was stunned and asked him, "Bishara, what happened to you?" He muttered, "You see, Master? You see?" I said, "You're begging? That's unbelievable!" He said, "How, then, am I to live? My uncle passed away." I said, "How about the foundry?" He said, "It's gone, a long time ago." I emptied my pocket and gave him the money I had, which was not much, and tried to hold back my tears. His sickly eyes welled up with tears as he said, "God bless you, Master, God bless you!" He dragged his feet and went away. I looked out for him at Jaffa Gate a few days later but did not find him. I saw a blind beggar, who usually had a spot in that area, so I went to him and asked him about Bishara. He said, "Bishara, the founder? The poor man died; may God have mercy on his soul. They say he died drunk. May God have mercy on him and on your parents."

I began to prepare myself for the occasion by saving the few piasters I was permitted to deduct from my weekly wages.

In that period of time, my attention was drawn to a man who passed by the foundry from time to time. When he passed, no one failed to notice him, for he was tall and awe inspiring, had a beautiful beard, and wore a green turban and a flowing black cloak. With one hand he gathered up the front of his cloak and with the other he leaned on a walking stick whose curved metallic handle shone as though it were made of gold. He walked with his head high and his chest forward, full of self-confidence and not without some haughtiness.

It so happened that my father was with us in the shop one hot morning when the turbaned man passed by and went down the road. We asked our neighbor, the blacksmith Abu al-Abd, about him, and he said, "This is Noor al-Deen, the astrologer and spiritualist. He lives nearby; above the door of his house there is a big sign, which you must have seen."

In fact, there was a group of houses of differing shapes on a slope near the foundry. One of them had a big sign as wide as the façade of the house, and it said "Noor al-Deen, Astrologer and Spiritualist." The words were between two large crescents with a star on the right and another on the left.

Abu al-Abd added, "He tells the future, heals neural diseases, reconciles hearts, and makes a barren woman give birth to twins!"

He looked at my father, at his heavy movements caused by Parkinson's disease, and at his trembling hand, and he said to him, "Try your luck with him, Abu Yusuf. If I were in your shoes, I would, by God."

My father turned to me and asked hesitantly, "What do you think?"

I said boldly, "Dad, I don't believe in cock-and-bull stories."

Abu al-Abd laughed and said before picking up his heavy hammer, "Do you consult a child regarding such matters, man?"

I returned to my work, and my father went away.

Two or three days later, my father came home happily. He said that, at long last, he was going to be healed in one month or two. He had visited the astrologer-spiritualist, who had set his mind at rest and given him the good tidings of his healing. The man had made him an amulet, which he showed us. Hung around his neck, it was in a black leather pouch almost stuck to his chest near his heart. The man had also given him a rare drug, the like of which he would never find in any pharmacy. My father took out a small bottle with green pills from his pocket. As he put one pill in his mouth, the mintlike smell of menthol spread in the air. We were happy with him for a couple of seconds, but then my brother Yusuf snatched away the bottle from my father and emptied the pills into his hand. He found they were a gelatinous kind of pastille that one took for a cold to relieve any accompanying throat inflammation. Yusuf himself had bought a metal box with about twenty such pills from the pharmacy for five piasters. He asked my father, "Tell the truth, Dad. How many piasters did this astrologer-physician charge you?"

My father answered, "Three pounds."

"Three pounds?!" exclaimed Yusuf. "We all work every day and don't earn as much as three pounds in a whole month. Are you crazy?"

My father said, "But a drug like this can't be found in the city. Besides, the astrologer is a knowledgeable person and wants to save me from this suffering. . . . Do you begrudge your father this amount and deem it too much?"

Yusuf said, "Daddy, my beloved. If he were able to heal you, I would give up my soul for you. . . . But don't you see that he is a quack who takes advantage of your suffering and psychological state? Come with me. . . . We'll go to him together and throw his sugary pills back to him. If he returns the three pounds, that's the end of that. Otherwise, I'll beat him up and expose him for what he is for all to see."

My brother accompanied my father, and they went out to the encounter. I followed them and waited at the top of the slope at my father's request, "lest we should make much of the matter." They descended the slope to the astrologer's door and knocked. Wearing his turban and cloak in the most awe-inspiring manner, the owner himself came out to them. I heard some noise, but it did not last long. The astrologer was obviously not prepared for situations of this kind, for I saw him take out something from his inner pocket and hand it to Yusuf. He returned the three pounds, and we returned home victoriously. We recalled the story of my father's cauterization with that horrible key, as well as other stories that were part of his despair and tenacity. And in a moment of anger and frustration, he took the amulet from around his neck and threw it on the floor.

I picked it up, tried to open it, but couldn't. I brought a pair of scissors, cut off the end of the amulet, and took from it the magic my father was promised: a white, foolscap paper on which squares were drawn, about forty of them. In each square, there was a letter of the alphabet or a star. The letters did not suggest any meaning. I had hoped it might at least be the Throne Verse of the Qur'an. But the astrologer-spiritualist was more clever than to write Qur'anic verses that everyone knew. Letters and stars, however, had a cryptic character and therein lay his magic. If we were to tell him what we had done, he would doubtlessly say that magic would lose its effect if its secret was uncovered.

■ ■ ■

I lost hope of receiving the school report, and as soon as I learned from Sharif that school had reopened, I got up early in the morning of the next day, had my breakfast with my brother, and eagerly hastened to the Rashidiyya School, as though I had an appointment with a beloved person.

I met my friends in the playground, and we were all happy to see one another after our absence during the summer months. The bell rang, and I stood in line in the hall with my friends who were going to the room of the sixth class. When we started moving forward and going upstairs to the classrooms under the supervision of Principal Arif al-Budayri and some teachers, the principal beckoned to me, and I went up to him. He said, "Go upstairs to my office and wait for me."

In the office, I saw others standing and waiting for the

principal. Soon, he came hurriedly, accompanied by a young man whom he seated on a chair near his desk. For some reason, he turned to me first and said in a sharp tone that shook me at once, "Jabra, you have no place with us. Go back home."

I was stunned, but I did not move from my place.

He repeated, "I said to you, you have no place with us. Please leave."

"But why, Sir?" I asked in an agitated, hoarse voice.

He turned to the young man at his right and said, "Najib, explain to him that one who behaves as he has done, does not deserve a place in my school."

Najib was embarrassed and said to me in an extremely gentle tone, "Sorry. You've heard what my father said. Please go back home."

I insisted, "What have I done?"

I imagined I had committed a reprehensible crime that I had concealed from people but that was now uncovered, and so I deserved punishment. However, I could not remember that I had done any act punishable with such severity.

Najib turned to his father and said almost in a whisper, "What did he do?"

The principal said, "On the last day of the examination period. . . ." He looked at me and added, "Do you remember?"

I said, "Yes. I came to the hall, although I was not required to take the examination."

"Nonsense," he said. "You were not required to take the examination but you were required to stay put in your seat until your classmates finished their examination."

"But I did stay for almost one hour," I said.

He angrily chided, "Do you count minutes with me? You had to stay until the end. But you ran away. . . . Now please, go back home."

He kicked me out of school for a reason that I found completely unjust. I left deeply hurt about losing the thing I loved most. I returned home, not knowing how I could return. Conflicting thoughts took hold of me: Was this the end of school for me? Would I return to the foundry, to be welcomed back by

Bishara and the prince? No! I would return to my school in Bethlehem. The principal there liked me, so did the teachers. They would rejoice at my return. But how could I go to and return from Bethlehem daily? By bus, of course. That would cost me two piasters per day. Two piasters! Where in the world would I get this amount? I had to go and return on foot every day. . . . I calculated the distance: eight kilometers, plus two more at least from the edge of the town to school. Multiplied by two, this made twenty kilometers every day.

As soon as I went down the courtyard stairs and entered our room, I flung myself down on the floor and started crying so violently that I could not stop. My father, mother, and grandmother gathered around me seeking to know the reason. I said to them, "The principal has kicked me out of school. . . . I want to return to Bethlehem."

My father kept insistently asking for more information, and I told him what the principal had said. He immediately took his walking stick and went out.

What could my father do? Had it been a question of a tire that had fallen into the deep valley, he would have gone down and retrieved it even though it might be in the depths of Hell, if retrieving it would save me from difficulty. The question now was related to a much more difficult problem: There were rules and regulations that I had seemingly broken, and there was the will of a man feared by everybody and not likely to relent or accept logical argument. What could my father do?

He went to a young monk named Father Butrus Sumi* who lived in the Convent of St. Mark in the Old City and was known for his moral courage and articulateness. He was originally a classmate of my brother Murad when he was a student at the Convent. The monk did not hesitate for a moment, and he accompanied my father to the Rashidiyya School to see the

---

*This monk was killed toward the end of May 1948 during the fierce fighting that took place inside the city walls of Jerusalem and that ended with the victory of the Palestinian fighters and the Arab army over the Zionist fighting force in the Old City, whereupon the Jews were expelled from it.

principal. The latter met them in a friendly and welcoming manner. When they sat down, the monk said, "My friend here, Mr. Principal, has a case in which he was unjustly treated, and I have no doubt that you will see that justice is done to him."

Mr. Budayri did not know who the monk's friend was when he said to him, "Please, go ahead."

My father began, "We have erred, and we beg for your forgiveness."

The principal said, "Please, speak."

My father repeated, "We have erred, and we beg for your forgiveness."

The principal said impatiently, "I understand, sir. Please, tell me your story."

My father said, "I have a son with you whose name is. . . ."

"Yes, yes," interrupted the principal. "I know the story. I sent him back home this morning."

My father explained, "It is as if you have killed him, and me too, Mr. Principal. . . . Meanwhile, I am as you see. . . ."

My father fell silent and the principal did not answer as he looked thoughtfully at my father. Suddenly he said, "Sayyid Ibrahim, you have dumbfounded me. You are a good-hearted man, and on account of your good heart, I'll forgive your son. Send him to me as soon as you go back home."

My father and the monk stood up and thanked him profusely as they shook his hand and said good-bye. "No, no," he said to my father. "Don't thank me. I am proud to see a man in as bad a condition as you are, who insists on educating his son."

That very morning, when my father returned to me and informed me of what had happened, I ran all the way to school and reached it out of breath before the morning session had ended. I saw the principal in the upper hall talking to some teachers. Shaking his finger at me, he immediately said to me, "By God, had it not been for your good-hearted father, I would have never changed my mind!"

I replied, "Thank you, sir."

He said, "Don't thank me. Thank your father. Hurry back to class."

I entered the classroom, not believing that I was not in a dream. The teacher, Ibrahim Tuqan, seated me next to a new student who had not been with us in the fifth class and whose name was Musa al-Su'udi. My greatest surprise was when the principal entered and the students stood up in respect and then sat down. He approached me with a folded paper in his hand and said, "Here is your report." And he went out.

With trembling fingers, I opened the paper, afraid of what I might see. Lo and behold, I was the second in Arabic, the first in English, the second in mathematics, and the first in history. My rank in class was the second.

■ ■ ■

When I was at the beginning of my thirteenth year, my sister, Susan, was very attached to our cat, Fulla. We had grown up with her, and we had brought her with us from Bethlehem and had saved her more than once from the hands of harsh people who did not want her to live. Several months after our move to Jawrat al-Unnab, Fulla disappeared one day, and we did not know what had happened to her. I returned from school, my head echoing with the verses that Ibrahim Tuqan had read to us in his admirable way from act 1 of Ahmad Shawqi's play *Majnun Layla* (*Layla's Mad Lover*) about Layla and the deer. The play (or the *riwaya* as Ahmad Shawqi had called it and as Arab people used to call any play and still do) had been published in the previous year and had recently reached Jerusalem. Ibrahim Tuqan, who used to transform the Arabic class into an hour of magic with his poetic sensibility, tenderness, and good sense of irony, did not abide by the prescribed materials or books. The play was always in his hand, along with other books, whenever he entered the classroom in those early days of the academic year, and he read it to us in successive periods, scene by scene.

> Qays saw a deer on a hill and called out to it.
> The deer lent him its ears, its horns touching the ground.
> Remnants of grass on its mouth dyed its lips with green.
> Its lovely neck and eyes reminded Qays of his own Layla.

As he yearned for her and ecstatically called her to mind,
The wolf crept to the deer from the valley and killed it.
It ate the deer's innards for lunch, but didn't enjoy it.
For Qays shot an arrow at the wolf and hit it fatally.

These were the verses echoing in my mind. How easy they were to remember by heart! On reaching home, I saw Susan (who was then about four years old) and my brother Issa sitting on the threshold at the entrance of the building. They were waiting to tell me that Fulla had gone astray. We started looking for her in the neighborhood, able as we were to recognize her among a thousand cats. We asked the neighbors and the passersby about her. I recited the verses I remembered about Layla and the deer to my brother and sister, and this added to Susan's grief for the cat. We returned home as she continued to cry over the lost Fulla, and I kept telling her that I would one day write a poem about "Susan and her straying cat."

Two or three days later, we woke up in the early morning to the sound of Fulla mewing beautifully outside the closed door. We opened the door for the cat, and Susan carried her on her chest crying, this time out of joy for her return.

However, that joy did not last long, for Fulla began to show signs of sickness. She moved with a heavy step and lost her appetite, while earlier she used to eat even cucumbers and tomatoes from our hands. The day we woke up and saw her lying dead near the door was a day of mourning for all of us, and especially for Susan. But her weeping and her tears were to no avail. In that fourth year of her life, she appeared to be angry and unable to understand this event. Why should Fulla die? Why? Why?

My mother said, "The poor cat became old. It died of old age. Do you know how old it was? Do you know how many mice it ate and how many rats it killed in its lifetime? Hundreds. . . ."

Out of love for Susan and out of respect for her wishes, we placed the dead cat in a cardboard box and took it to the top of the rocky hill facing the entrance of our building. We buried it there and marked the place with a pile of stones.

Later on, Susan often repeated the following verses from *Majnun Layla,* and Yusuf, Issa, and I repeated them with her, the cat having been transformed in them into the deer or vice versa:

> We dug a grave for the deer and we buried it.
> We prayed over the dead body and shed tears on it.
> Join me, and Layla too, and say, "God's mercy be on it."

21

And so I became thirteen years old and stood at the threshold of the discoveries that would be realized in the following years of adolescence. The beautiful city of Jerusalem was there for me to discover, neighborhood by neighborhood, stone by stone, the old part and the new, its past and its present. There were also the Egyptian magazines which, every week, brought us knowledge, humor, and news of Cairo's political conflicts and literary battles. There were the books that we obtained with difficulty, by trickery, and by sacrifice: ancient biographies, stories, novels, poetry collections, histories. There were also the new teachers who had just returned from the universities of the world and who imbued us with the love of knowledge. There were the delightful girls, whom I began to see every-where as if they were walking in an endless dream. Or was it I who was dream walking with them and deprived of sleep? I wrote long letters trying in vain to combine dream and reality.

There was also drawing in pencil and painting in water-colors, which made me see people and things sharply and radi-antly. There was music too: the lute, the guitar, and the violin, which I attempted to teach myself to play for a while until I could not go any further because there was nobody to instruct me; but I kept on with the accordion, which Yusuf paid for in small installments and which opened for us a whole universe of uproar and merriment. Then there were the classical music records and my infatuation with Beethoven that mostly came to me from a friend, whose father was a peddler who carried a large glass box on his chest all day long and sold popcorn in paper cones. This friend of mine worked as a goldsmith for an Armenian jeweler in the Old City and had learned the principles of music and was a talented musician. On his violin, he played some of Beethoven's pieces from written music, moved his long and delicate fingers on the strings with almost inhuman accuracy and speed and imagined that Beethoven was reincarnated in him because he bore a resemblance to him. He collected books about him, of which he could read only a few lines because they were all in English.

There was also the Arab College with its great dean, Professor Ahmad Samih al-Khalidi, who had a stentorian voice and a strong presence. He turned his educational theories into a way of life and so would accept nothing from his students but the pursuit of knowledge and distinction as a relentless patriotic tenet. At the new site of the college on Mount al-Mukabbir which was open to all the world's ideas blown there on the four winds, we read and studied with passion and perseverance all day long, and then all night to the point of sickness. Professor Al-Khalidi was the one who finally selected me to be sent on a fellowship to study abroad.

There was also increasing political consciousness; there were the demonstrations; there was the general strike of 1936, and the rebellion that continued for three years afterward until the outbreak of the Second World War. There were the long walks, the tireless hikes for miles every day, which we took because our homes were not capable of holding our endless, explosive discussions, which even the whole wide world could hardly contain.

And there was the devastating sorrow that hit us suddenly in 1938 with the death of my sister at the age of nine, who lay with her long maroon hair flowing on her shoulders and chest like that of the angels, and her skin which resembled rose petals on a dewy morning. Not even death could take away the red of her cheeks and lips.

Then there were the beginnings of writing and translation,

with all their pleasures and difficulties. And there was also the teaching job at a miserable elementary school for a few months, after which I prepared myself to travel to England on scholarship.

These and many others are chapters of an autobiography which would require great patience to narrate, needing—as they do—to dwell on the delights, the pains, and the raptures that prepared me for a long absence from home and a great upheaval in the way of life in evergreen England, which in those days resounded with bombs, with the clamor of students constantly moving, drinking, and arguing and of female students with bright eyes and luscious lips. It resounded with the shouts of books that I began to buy by the dozen, the shouts I lived with day after day, hour after hour, together with an inner shout, intensifying within me at one moment to the point of tears and madness, and at another to the point of stupor and silence.

Baghdad, May 1986.